The Story of Louis Riel

The Rebel Chief

J. E. Collins

Alpha Editions

This edition published in 2024

ISBN : 9789362927019

Design and Setting By
Alpha Editions
www.alphaedis.com
Email - info@alphaedis.com

As per information held with us this book is in Public Domain.
This book is a reproduction of an important historical work. Alpha Editions uses the best technology to reproduce historical work in the same manner it was first published to preserve its original nature. Any marks or number seen are left intentionally to preserve its true form.

Contents

CHAPTER I. .... - 1 -

CHAPTER II. .... - 5 -

CHAPTER III. .... - 15 -

CHAPTER IV. .... - 24 -

CHAPTER V. .... - 29 -

CHAPTER VI. .... - 38 -

CHAPTER VII. .... - 46 -

CHAPTER VIII. .... - 59 -

CHAPTER IX. .... - 78 -

CHAPTER X. .... - 82 -

CHAPTER XI. .... - 88 -

CHAPTER XII. .... - 92 -

CHAPTER XIII. .... - 97 -

CHAPTER XIV. .... - 101 -

CHAPTER XV .... - 103 -

THE TRIAL AND EXECUTION OF LOUIS RIEL .... - 114 -

SECOND DAY OF THE TRIAL. ....- 119 -

THIRD DAY OF THE TRIAL. ....- 124 -

MEDICAL TESTIMONY. ....- 128 -

RIEL'S ADDRESS TO THE JURY. ....- 129 -

THIRD DAY'S PROCEEDINGS. ....- 133 -

THE VERDICT. ....- 134 -

THE PRISONER'S SPEECH..- 135 -

THE SENTENCE. ....- 137 -

AN APPEAL...- 138 -

NEW TRIAL REFUSED...- 139 -

RIEL'S EXECUTION. ....- 140 -

END..- 141 -

CHAPTER I.

Along the banks of the Red River, over those fruitful plains brightened with wild flowers in summer, and swept with fierce storms in the winter-time, is written the life story of Louis Riel. Chance was not blind when she gave as a field to this man's ambition the plains whereon vengeful Chippewas and ferocious Sioux had waged their battles for so many centuries; a country dyed so often with blood that at last Red River came to be its name. But while our task is to present the career of this apostle of insurrection and unrest; stirred as we may be to feelings of horror for the misery, the tumult, the terror and the blood of which he has been the author, we must not neglect to do him, even him, the justice which is his right.

He is not, as so many suppose, a half-breed, moved by the vengeful, irresponsible, savage blood in his veins. Mr. Edward Jack, [Footnote: I cannot make out what Mr. Jack's views are respecting Riel. When I asked him, he simply turned his face toward the sky and made some remark about the weather, I know that he has strong French proclivities, though the blood of a Scottish bailie is in his veins.] of New Brunswick, who is well informed on all Canadian matters, hands me some passages which he has translated from M. Tasse's book on Canadians in the North West; and from these I learn that Riel's father, whose name also was Louis, was born at the island of La Crosse, in the North-West Territories. This parent was the son of Jean Baptiste Riel, who was a French Canadian and a native of Berthier (*en haut*). His mother, that is the rebel's grandmother, was a Franco-Montagnaise Metis. From this it will be seen that instead of being a "half breed," Louis Riel is only one-eighth Indian, or is, if we might use the phrase employed in describing a mixture of Ethiopian and Caucasian blood, an Octoroon.

Nay, more than this, we have it shown that our rebel can lay claim to no small share of respectability, as that word goes. During the summer of 1822, Riel's father, then in his fifth year, was brought to Canada by his parents, who caused the ceremony of baptism to be performed with much show at Berthier. In 1838 M. Riel *pere* entered the service of the Hudson Bay Company, and left Lower Canada, where he had been attending school, for the North-West. He was stationed at Rainy Lake, but did not care for his occupation. He returned, therefore, to civilization and entered as a novice in the community of the Oblat Fathers, where he remained for two years. There was a strong yearning for the free, wild life of the boundless prairies in this man, and Red River, with its herds of roaming buffalo, its myriads of duck, and geese and prairie hens, began to beckon him home again. He followed his impulse and departed; joining the Metis hunters in their great biennial campaigns against the herds, over the rolling prairie. Many a buffalo fell upon the plain with Louis Riel's arrow quivering in his flank; many a feast was held around the giant pot at which no hunter received honours so marked as stolid male, and olive-skinned, bright-eyed, supple female, accorded him. Surfeited for the time of the luxury of the limitless plain, Riel took rest; and then a girl with the lustrous eyes of Normandy began to smile upon him, and to besiege his heart with all her mysterious force of coquetry. He was not proof; and the hunter soon lay entangled in the meshes of the brown girl of the plains. In the autumn of 1843 he married her. Her name was Julie de Lagimodiere, a daughter of Jean Baptiste de Lagimodiere.

Louis *pere* was now engaged as a carder of wool; and having much ability in contrivance he constructed a little model of a carding mill which, with much enthusiasm, he exhibited to some officers of the Hudson Bay Company. But the Company, though having a great body, possessed no soul, and the disappointed inventor returned to his waiting wife with sorrow in his eyes. He next betook himself to the cultivation of a farm upon the banks of the little Seine; and his good, patient wife, when the autumn came, toiled with him all day, with her sickle among the sheaves.

Tilling the soil proved too laborious, and he determined to erect a grist mill; but the stream that ran through the clayey channel of the *Seine petite* was too feeble to turn the ponderous wheels. So he was obliged to move twelve miles to the east, where flowed another small stream bearing the aesthetic name "Grease River." This was not large enough either for his purposes, so with stupendous enterprise he cut a canal nine miles long, and through it decoyed the waters of the little Seine into the arms of the "Greasy" paramour. At this mill was ground the grain that grew for many a mile around; and in a little while Louis Riel became known as the most enterprising and important settler in Red River. But he was not through all his career a man of peace. The most deadly feud had grown up through many long years between the Hudson Bay Company and the Metis settled upon their territory; and it is only bald justice to say that the, reprisals of the half-breeds, the revolts, the hatred of everything in official shape, were not altogether undeserved. Louis Riel was at the head of many a jarring discord. How such an unfortunate condition grew we shall see later on, and we may also be able to determine if there are any shoulders upon which we can lay blame for the murder and misery that since have blighted one of the fairest portions of Canada.

Louis Riel the elder was in due time blessed with a son, the same about whom it is our painful duty to write this little book. Estimating at its fullest the value of education, the father was keenly anxious for an opportunity to send *Louis fils* to a school; but fortune had not been liberal with him in later years, though the sweat was constantly upon his brow, and his good wife's fingers were never still. This son had unusual precocity, and strangers who looked upon him used to say that a great fire slumbered in his eye. He was bright, quick and piquant; and it is said that it was impossible to know the lad and not be pleased with his person and manners. One important eye had observed him many a time; and this was the great ecclesiastical dignitary of Red River, Monseigneur Tache. He conceived a strong affection for the lad and resolved to secure for him a sound education. His own purse was limited, but there was a lady whom he knew upon whose bounty he could count. I give the following extract, which I translate from M. Tasse's book, and I write it in italics that it may be the more clearly impressed upon the reader's mind when he comes to peruse the first story of blood which shall be related: *The father's resources did not permit him to undertake the expense of this education, but His Grace Archbishop Tache having been struck with the intellectual precocity of Louis, found a generous protector of proverbial munificence for him in the person of Madame Masson, of Terrebonne.* In later years it was reserved to the same bishop to go out as a mediator between Government and a band of rebels which had at its head a man whose hands were reddened with the blood of a settler. This rebel and murderer was the same lad upon whom the bishop had lavished his affection and his interest.

Louis, the elder, was travelling upon the plain, when he met his son, bound for the civilized East, to enter upon his studies. He had pride in the lad, and said to his companions that one day he knew he would have occasion to glory in him. They said good-bye, the father seasoning the parting with wholesome words of advice, the son with filial submission receiving them, and storing them away in his heart. This was their last parting, and their last speaking. Before the son had been long at his studies he learned that his father was dead. His nature was deeply affectionate, and the painful intelligence overwhelmed him for many days. At school he was not distinguished for brilliancy, but his tutors observed that he had solid parts, and much intellectual subtlety. He was not a great favourite among his class-mates generally, because his manners were shy and reserved, and he shrank from, rather than courted, the popularity and leadership which are the darling aims of so many lads in their school-days. Yet he had many friends who were warmly attached to him; and to these he returned an equal affection. One of his comrades was stricken down with a loathsome and fatal malady, and all his comrades fled in fear away from his presence. But Louis Riel, the "half-breed," as the boys knew him, bravely went to the couch of his stricken friend, nursing, and bestowing all his attention and affection upon him, and offering consoling words. It is related that when the last moments came, the sufferer arose, and flinging his arms around Louis' neck, poured out his thanks and besought heaven to reward him. Then he fell backwards and died.

Frequently young Riel's school-mates would ask him, "What do you intend doing when you leave school? Will you stay here, or do you go out again into the wilderness among the savages?"

His eye would lighten with indignation at hearing the word "savages" applied to his people. "I will go out to the Red River," he would reply, to follow in the footsteps of my father. He has been a benefactor of our people, and I shall seek to be their benefactor too. When I tire of work, I can take my gun and go out for herds upon the plains with our people, whom you call "savages." I know not what you mean when you say "savages." We speak French as you do; our hearts are as kind, as noble, and as true as yours. When one of our people is in affliction the others give him sympathy and help. We are bound together by strong ties of fraternity; there is no jealousy among us, no tyranny of caste, but we all live in peace and love as the sisters and brothers in one great household. My eye deceives me if like this live you. You are divided into envious, brawling factions, each one of which tries to injure, and blight the reputation of the other. If one of you fall upon evil times he is left without the sympathy and succour of the others. In politics and in social grades you are divided, and in every respect you are such that I should mourn the day when our peaceable, simple, contented people on the banks of the Red River should in any respect choose your civilization for their model.

He often spoke of a burning desire which he had to be a political as well as a social leader in the Colony of Red River. He frequently, likewise, muttered dark threats against the overbearing policy and dark injustice of "The Great Monopoly," as he used to characterize the Hudson Bay Company. Occasionally he would burst out into passionate words like these:

"They treat us as they would blood thirsty savages upon the plains. They spurn us with their feet as dogs, and then they spit upon us. They mock at our customs, they regard with contempt that which to us is sacred and above price. They are not even deterred by the virtue of our women. Now witness, you God who made all men, the white man and the savage, I will, if the propitious day ever come, strike in vengeance, and my blow will be with an iron hand, whose one smiting shall wipe out all the injustice and the dishonour."

Filled with these sentiments, when his school days came to an end, he packed his portmanteaus and took his way by stage and boat for the region that not many years hence was to ring and shudder with his name.

CHAPTER II.

Long before the vision of a confederation of the British Provinces entered into the brain of any man, Lord Selkirk, coming to the wilds of North America, found a tract of country fertile in soil, and fair to look upon. He arrived in this unknown wilderness when it was summer, and all the prairie extending over illimitable stretches till it was lost in the tranquil horizon, was burning with the blooms of a hundred varieties of flowers. Here the "tiger rose," like some savage queen of beauty, rose to his knees and breathed her sultry balm in his face. Aloof stood the shy wild rose, shedding its scent with delicate reserve; but the wild pea, and the convolvulus, and the augur flower, and the insipid daisy, ran riot through all the grass land, and surfeited his nostrils with their sweets. Here and there upon the mellow level stood a clump of poplars or white oaks, prim, like virgins without suitors, with their robes drawn close about them; but when over the unmeasured plain the wind blew, they bowed their heads: as if saluting the stranger who came to found a colony in the wilderness of which they were sentinels. Here too, in the hush, for the first time, the planter's ear heard a far-off, nigh indistinct, sound of galloping thunder. He knew not what it meant, and his followers surmised that it might be the tumult of some distant waterfall, borne hither now because a storm was at hand, and the denser air was a better carrier of the sound. And while they remained wondering what it could be, for the thunder was ever becoming louder, and,

"Nearer clearer, deadlier than before"

Lo! out of the west came what seemed as a dim shadow moving across the plain. With bated breath they watched the dark mass moving along like some destroying tempest with ten thousand devils at its core. Chained to the ground with a terrible awe they stood fast for many minutes till at last in the dim light, for the gloaming had come upon the plains, they see eye-balls that blaze like fire, heads crested with rugged, uncouth horns and shaggy manes; and then snouts thrust down, flaring nostrils, and rearing tails.

My God, a buffalo herd, and we'll be trampled to death," almost shrieked one of the Earl's followers.

"Peace! keep cool! Up, up instantly into these trees!" and the word was obeyed as if each man was an instrument of the leader's will. Beyond, in the south-east, a full moon, luscious seeming as some ripened, mellow fruit, was rising, and the yellow light was all over the plain. Then the tremendous mass, headed by maddened bulls, with blazing eyes and foaming nostrils, drove onward toward the south, like an unchained hurricane. Some of the terrified beasts ran against the trees, crushing horns and skull, and fell prone upon the plain, to be trampled into jelly by the hundreds of thousands in the rear. The tree upon which the earl had taken refuge received many a shock from a crazed bull; and it seemed to the party from the tree-branches as if all the face of the plains was being hurled toward the south in a condition of the wildest turmoil. Hell itself let loose could present no such spectacle as this myriad mass of brute life sweeping over the lonely plain under the wan, elfin light of the new-risen moon. Clouds of steam, wreathing itself into spectral shapes of sullen aspect, rose from the dusky, writhing mass, and the flaming of more than ten thousand eyeballs in the gloom presented a picture more terrible than ever came into the imagination of the writer of the Inferno. The spectacle, as observed by those some twenty feet from the ground, might be likened somewhat to a turbulent sea when a sturdy tide sets against the storm, and the mad waves tumble hither and thither, foiled, and impelled, yet for all the confusion and obstruction moving in one direction with a sweep and a force that no power could chain. Circling among and around the strange, dusk clouds of steam that went up from the herd were scores of turkey buzzards, their obscene heads bent downward, their sodden eyes gleaming with expectancy. Well they knew that many a gorgeous feast awaited them wherever boulder, tree, or swamp lay in the path of the mighty herd. At last the face of the prairie had ceased its surging; no lurid eyeball-light gleamed out of the dusk; and the tempest of cattle had passed the *voyageurs* and went rolling out into the unbounded stretches of the dim, yellow plain.

The morrow's sun revealed a strange spectacle. The great amplitude of rich, green grasses, warmed and beautified by the petals of flowers was as a ploughed field. The herbage had been literally crushed into mire, and this the innumerable hoofs had churned up with the soft, rich, dark soil of the prairie. The leguminous odours from decaying clover, and rank, matted masses of wild pease, the feverish exhalations of the tiger-lily, and of the rich blooded "buffalo lilac," together with the dank, earthy smell from the broken sod, were disagreeable and oppressive. Lord Selkirk's heart sank within him at seeing the ruin.

"I fear me," he said, "to plant a colony here. A herd of these beasts coming upon a settlement would be worse than ten thousand spears." But some of his guides had before seen the impetuous rushing of the herds, and they assured him that this might not occur again in this portion of the prairie for a quarter of a century to come.

"At any rate," they persisted, "the buffalo keeps away from regions that send up chimney-smoke. The chief regret by-and-by will be that the herds will not come near enough to us." And the Earl was reassured and proceeded with the steps preliminary to founding the colony. It need not be said that the place we have been describing was the prairie on the banks of the Red River.

In a little while ships bearing numbers of sturdy Scotchmen began to cross the sea bound for this famous colony, where the land was ready for the plough, and mighty herds of wild cattle grazed knee-deep among gorgeous flowers and sweet grasses. They brought few white women with them, the larger number being young men who had bade their "Heeland" lassies good-bye with warm kisses, promising to come back for them when they had built homesteads for themselves in the far away wilds of the West.

But when Lord Selkirk planted here his sturdy Scotchmen, wild beasts and game were not the only inhabitants of the plains. The Crees, a well-built, active, war-loving race, had from ages long forgotten roamed over these interminable meadows, fishing in the streams, and hunting buffalo. Here and there was to be found one of their "towns," a straggling congregation of tents made of the skins of the buffalo. Beautiful, dark-skinned girls, in bare brown, little feet, sat through the cool of evening in the summer days sewing beads upon the moccasins of their lovers, while the wrinkled dame limped about, forever quarrelling with the dogs, performing the household duties.

But the Crees liked not the encroachment upon their territories by these foreign men with pale faces; and they held loud pow-wows, and brandished spears, and swept their knives about their heads till their sheen gleamed many miles over the prairie. Then preparing their paint they set out to learn from the pale-faced chief what was his justification for the invasion.

"You cannot take lands without war and conquest," were the words of a young chief with a nose like a hawk's beak, and an eye like the eagle's, to Lord Selkirk. "You did not fight us; therefore you did not conquer us. How comes it then that you have our lands?"

"Are you the owners of this territory?" calmly enquired the nobleman.

"We are; no one else is the owner."

"But I shall shew you that from two standpoints, first from my own, and afterwards from yours, it belongs not to you. Firstly, it belongs to our common Sovereign, the King of England. You belong to him; so likewise do the buffalo that graze upon the plains, and the fishes that swim in the rivers. Therefore our great and good Sovereign sayeth unto me, his devoted subject, 'Go you forth into my territories in the North of America, and select there a colony whereon to plant any of my faithful children who choose to go thither.' I have done so. Then, since you hold possession of these plains only by the bounty and sufferance of our good father the King, how can you object to your white brethren coming when they were permitted so to do?"

Ugh; that was only the oily-tongued talk of the pale-faces. While seeming to speak fair, and smooth, and wise, their tongues were as crooked as the horn of the mountain-goat. Yet no chief could answer the Earl's contention, and they looked from one to another with some traces of confusion and defeat upon their faces.

"But," continued Lord Selkirk, in the same grave and firm voice, "from your own standpoint you are not the proprietors of this territory. The Saulteux, with whom you wage your constant wars, have been upon these plains as long as you. In times of peace you have intermarried with them, and I now find in your wigwams many a squaw obtained from among the villages of your rivals."

Ugh! They could not deny this. It was evident from their silence and the abject way in which they glanced from one to another that the case had gone against them.

"But there is no reason for your jealousy or your hostility," Lord Selkirk continued; "our people come among you, not as conquerors, but as brothers. They shall not molest you but quietly till the fields and raise their crops. Instead of showing unfriendliness, I think you should take them by the hand and welcome them as brothers." These words at last prevailed, and the Crees put by their war paint, and came among the whites and offered them fish and buffalo steak.

Thus was the colony founded. The grain grew well, and there was abundance in the new settlement, save that at intervals an army of locusts would come out of the west and destroy every green leaf. Then the settlers' needs were sore, and they were obliged to subsist upon roots and what fell to them from the chase.

Many years rolled on, and the sturdy Scotch settlers had driven their roots fast into the ground. One alone of all the number who had kissed good-bye to his Scottish sweetheart returned to redeem his pledge. For the rest they soon forgot the rosy cheeks and bright blue eyes that they had left behind them, in the pleasures of the chase upon the plain, and the interest in their wide acres. But these perhaps were not the only reasons why they had forgotten their vows to the Scottish girls. Among the Crees were many beautiful maidens, with large, velvety eyes, black as the night when no moon is over the prairie, and shy as a fawn's. When first the white man came amongst them the girls were bashful; and when he went into the Crees' tent they would shrink away hiding their faces. But it soon became apparent that the shyness was not indifference; indeed many a time when the Scotch hunter passed a red man's tent he saw a pair of eyes looking languishingly after him. Little by little the timidity began to disappear, and sometimes the brown-skinned girls came in numbers to the white man's dwelling, and submitted themselves to be taught how to dance the cotillion and the eight-hand reel. Then followed the wooing among the flowery prairies; and the white men began to pledge their troths to the dusky girls. Many a brave hunter who had a score of scalps to dangle from his belt, sought, but sought in vain, a kind glance from some beautiful maiden of his tribe, who before the pale faces came would have deemed great indeed the honour of becoming the spouse of a warrior so distinguished. Jealousy began to fill the hearts of the Crees, but the mothers and wives, and the daughters too, were constant mediators, and never ceased to exert themselves for peace.

"When," said they, "the white-faces first came among us, our chiefs and our young men all cried out, 'O they deem themselves to be a better race than we; they think their white blood is better than our red blood. They will not mingle with us although they will join with us in hunting our wild meat, or eating it after it has fallen to our arrow or spear. They will not consider one of our daughters fit for marriage with one of them; because it would blend their blood with our blood.' Now, O you chiefs and young men, that which you at the first considered a hardship if it did not come to pass, has come to pass, and yet you complain. 'The whites are above marrying our daughters,' you first cry; now you plan revenge because they want to marry, and do marry them." The arguments used by the women were too strong, and the brawny, eagle-eyed hunters were compelled to mate themselves with the ugly girls of the tents. It is asserted by some writers on the North-West that the beauty observed in the Metis women in after years was in great part to be attributed to the fact that the English settlers took to wife only the most beautiful of the Indian girls. Now and again too, the canny Scotch lad, with his gun on his shoulder and his retriever at his heel, would walk through a Saulteux settlement. The girls here were still shyer than their Cree cousins, but they were not a whit less lovely. They were not dumpy like so many Indian girls, but were slight of build, and willowy of motion. Their hair was long and black, but it was as fine as silk, and shone like the plumage of a blackbird. There was not that oily swarthiness in the complexion, which makes so many Indian women hideous in the eyes of a connoisseur of beauty; but the cheeks of these girls were a pale olive, and sometimes, when they were excited, a faint tinge of rose came out like the delicate pink flush that appears in the olive-grey of the morning. And these maidens, too, began to cast languishing eyes upon the pale-faced stranger; and sighed all the day while they sewed fringe upon their skirts and beads upon their moccasins. Their affections now were not for him who showed the largest number of wolves' tongues or enemies' scalps, but for the gracious stranger with his gentle manners and winning ways. They soon began to put themselves in his way when he came to shoot chicken or quail among the grasses; would point out to him passes leading around the swamps, and inform him where he might find elk or wild turkey. Then with half shy, yet half coquettish airs, and a lurking tenderness in their great dusk hazel eyes, they would twist a sprig off a crown of golden rod, and with their dainty little brown fingers pin it upon the hunter's coat. With shy curiosity they would smoothe the cloth woven in Paisley, forming in their minds a contrast between its elegance and that of the coats of their own red gallants made of the rough skin of the wolf or the bison. So it came to pass that in due season most of the pretty girls among the Jumping Indians had gone with triumph and great love in their hearts from the wigwam of their tribe to be the wives of the whites in their stately dwellings.

In this way up-grew the settlement of Red River; by such intermarriages were the affections of the red men all over the plains, from the cold, gloomy regions of the North to the mellow plains of the South, won by their pale-faced neighbours. The savages had not shut their ears to what their women had so eloquently urged, and they would say:

"The cause of these pale people is our cause; their interests are our interests; they have mingled their flesh and blood with ours; we shall be their faithful brothers to the death." It was this fact, not the wisdom of government Indian agents, nor the heaven-born insight of government itself into the management of tribes that so long preserved peace and good will throughout our North-West Territories. It was for this reason that enemies of government in the Republic could say after they had revealed the corruption of Red Cloud and Black Rock agents:

"Observe the Canadian tribes, mighty in number, and warlike in their nature. They fight not, because they have been managed with wisdom and humanity. There is no corruption among the accredited officials; there is no sinister dealing towards them by the government." We do not charge our officials with corruption, neither do we believe that their administration has been feeble;—on the whole our attitude towards the Indian people has been fair; our policy has revealed ordinary sense,—and not much brilliancy. Probably half a dozen level-headed wood-choppers, endowed with authority to deal with the tribes, could have acquitted themselves as well; perhaps they might not have done so well, and it is probable that they might have exhibited a better showing.

It was in this settlement that in after years appeared Louis Riel *pere*. For some generations the Hudson Bay Company had carried on an extensive trade in peltry, and numbers of their *employes* were French peasants or *coureurs de bois*. Thousands of these people were scattered here and there over the territories; and they began to turn loving eyes toward the rich meadows along the banks of the Red River. Some of these had for wives squaws whom they had wooed and won during their engagement in the peltry trade. These finding that other whites had taken Indian girls for brides, felt drawn towards the new settlement by sentiments stronger than those of mere interest. Numbers of unmarried French took up farms in the new colony, and soon fell captive to the charms of the Cree girls. Now and again the history of the simple-hearted Scots was repeated; and a *coureur* was presently seen to bring a shy, witching Saulteux maiden from the tents of the Jumping Indians. But the French, it must be said, were not so *dilettante* in their taste for beauty as were their Scottish brethren; yet, as a rule, their wives were the prettiest girls in the tribes —after, of course, "braw John" had been satisfied—for an ugly maiden was content to have an Indian for her lord; and she tried no arts, plucked no bouquets from the prairie flowers, beaded no moccasins, and performed no tender little offices to catch the heart of the white man.

"Pale face gets all the pretty squaws; suppose we must take 'em ugly ones. Ugh!" This was the speech, and the true speech of many a chief, or lion-hearted young man of the tribes under the new order at Red River.

This may seem hard to the poor Indian, but perhaps it was just as well. It would have, indeed, been worse had the handsome maiden given her hand to the dusky Red, and afterwards, wooed by blue eyes, given her heart where her hand could never go. And the Indian woman is no better and no worse than her kind, no matter what the colour be. Happier, then, is the lot of the Indian with his homely affectionate wife, than with a bride with roses in her cheek, and sunlight in her eye, who cannot resist the pleading eye and the outstretched arms of one whose wooing is unlawful, and the result of which can be nought but wrong and misery.

The population grew and comforts increased till eighteen or twenty thousand souls could be reckoned in the colony. The original whites had disappeared, and no face was to be seen but that of a Metis in any of the cosy dwellings in the settlement. These people had not yet learnt that amongst the whites, whose blood knew no alloy, they were regarded as a debased sort, and unfit socially to mix with those who had kept their race free from taint. The female fruitage of the mixture lost nothing by acquiring some of the Caucasian stock, but the men, in numerous cases, seemed to be inferior for the blending. In appearance they were inane, in speech laconic; they were shy in manners, and reserved, to boorishness, while in intellectual alertness they were inferior to the boisterous savage, or the shrewd, dignified white. But the woman perpetuated the shy, winning coyness of her red mother, and the arts, and somewhat of the refinements of her white father. The eye was not so dusk; it gleamed more: as if the ray from a star had been shot through it. There was the same olive cheek; but it was not so tawny, for the dawn of the white blood had appeared in it. She gained in symmetry too, being taller than her red mother, while she preserved the soft, willowy motion of the prairie-elk.

But the women were not good housekeepers; and many a traveller has gone into the house of a Metis and seen there a bride witchingly beautiful, with her hair unkempt and disordered about her shoulders, her boots unlaced, and her stocking down revealing her bare, exquisitely-turned ankle.

"A Cinderella!" he would exclaim, "but, by heaven, I swear, a thousand times more lovely!" If she had a child it would likely be found sprawling among the coals, and helping itself to handfuls of ashes. The little creature would be sure to escape the suspicion of ever having been washed. Ask the luminous-eyed mother for anything, for a knife to cut your tobacco, for a cup to get a drink of water, and the sweet sloven would be obliged to ransack two-thirds of the articles of the house to find what you sought.

The dresses worn by herself, as well as by her husband or her brother, would not be less astonishing to the unaccustomed eye. The men wear a common blue capote a red belt and corduroy trousers. This, however, soon became the costume of every male in Red River, whether Metis or new-come Canadian. There, is however, a distinction in the manner of wearing. Lest the Canadian should be taken for a Metis he wears the red belt over the capote, while the half-breed wears it beneath. The women are fond of show, and like to attire themselves in dark skirts, and crimson bodices. Frequently, if the entire dress be dark, they tie a crimson or a magenta sash around their handsomely shapen waists; and they put a cap of some denomination of red upon their heads. Such colours, it need not be said, add to their beauty, and it is by no means uncertain that this is the reason why they adopt these colours. Some writers say that their love of glaring colours is derived from the savage side of their natures; but the Metis women have an artistic instinct of their own, and being for the greater part coquettes, it may very safely be said that according to the fitness of things is it that they attire themselves. But they are not able to shake off the superstitions of their race. If the young woman soon to be a mother, sees a hawk while crossing the fields in the morning, she comes home and tells among her female friends that her offspring is to be a son; and they all know that he is to be fleet and enduring in the chase, and that he will have the eyes of a hunter chief. But if a shy pigeon circle up from the croft, and cross her path, she sighs and returns not back to relate the omen; and it is only in undertones that her nearest friend learns a week afterwards that the promised addition to the household is to be a girl. The appearance of other birds and beasts, under similar circumstances, are likewise tokens; and though boys would be born, and girls too, if all the hawks and pigeons, and foxes and wild geese, and every other presaging bird and beast of the plains had fallen to the gun of huntsman and "sport," they cling to the belief; and the superstition will only die with the civilization that begat it. Many of the customs of their red mothers they still reverently perpetuate; but they are for all this deeply overlaid with Canadianism. Of all the women on the face of the earth, they are the greatest gossips.

Not in their whole nature is there any impulse so strong as the love to talk. Therefore, when the morning's meal is ended, the pretty mother laces the boots around her shapely little ankles, puts her blanket about her, and sallies out to one of her friend's houses for the morning's gossip. In speaking of her dress, I neglected to state that although the Metis woman had for gown the costliest fabric ever woven in Cashmere, she would not be content, on the hottest summer day, in walking twenty paces to her neighbour's door, unless she had this blanket upon her. The hateful looking garment is the chief relic of her barbaric origin, and despite the desire which she always manifests to exhibit her personal charms at their best, she has no qualms in converting herself into a hideous, repulsive squaw, with this covering. If she be of a shy nature, she will cover her head with this garment when a stranger enters her abode; and many a curious visitor who has heard of the bright eyes and olive cheeks of the half-breed woman is sorely disappointed when drawing near to her on the prairie path, or in the village street, to see her pull the hideous blanket over her face while he passes her by. Not always will she do this, for the wild women of the plains, and the half breed beauties, find a strong charm in strange faces; and after she has received some little attentions, and a few trinkets or trifles, she will be ready enough to appoint a tryst upon the flowery prairie, under the mellow moon.

We might forgive her for all this, if she could but restrain her tongue. From morn to noon, from noon to dewy eve, this unruly member goes on prattling about every conceivable thing, especially the affairs of her neighbours. We have seen that she goes out after she has eaten her breakfast; and she returns not till her appetite begins to be oppressive. She will then kiss her dusky little offspring, who, during her absence, has likely enough tried to stuff himself with coals, and then played with the pigs. In the evening one is pretty certain to find at some house a fiddler and a dancing party, which ends with a bountiful supper; though frequently, if the refreshments include whiskey, the party terminates with a regulation "Irish row." At nearly every such dance there is a white lad or two, and they are certain to monopolize the attention and the kisses of the prettiest girls. As the Indian had to sit by and see the white man come and take away the most beautiful of the wild girls, so too must the half-breed bear with meekness the preference of the Metis belle for the Caucasian stranger.

The morals of the women are not over good, nor can they be said to be very bad. Amongst each other their virtue reaches a standard as high as that which prevails in our Canadian community. It is when the women are brought into contact with the white men that this standard lowers. Then comes the temptation, the sin, the domestic heartburnings, and the hatred towards those who tempted to the fall.

The half-breed young men are fatally fond of show. The highest aim of their social existence seems to be to possess a dashing horse or two, and to drive a cariole. It is stated, on excellent authority, that a young man who wishes to figure as a *beau*, and to get the smiles of the pretty girls, will sometimes sell all his useful possessions to purchase a horse and cariole.

But it must not be supposed that this sort of spirit pervades the entire community. A large portion of the people are thrifty and frugal, and maintain themselves by continuous, well-directed toil.

The French half breeds profess the Roman Catholic religion, and they have a number of churches. At the head of the Roman communion is Archbishop Tache, of St. Boniface. This is the gentleman who provided the munificence for Louis Riel's education. He is the same bishop whose name so many hundreds of thousands of our people cannot recall without bitterness and indignation.

CHAPTER III.

Such, then, was the condition of Red River before the person who is the subject of this book appeared upon the scenes. But perhaps it is as well that I should relate one occurrence which fanned into bright flame the smouldering embers of discord between the half-breeds and their white neighbours. An officer of the Hudson Bay Company, living at an isolated post, had two daughters. As they began to arrive toward young-womanhood he was anxious that they should have an education, in order that they might, in proper season, be able to take their position in society. There were good schools at Red River, and thither the officer sent his daughters, placing them under the care of a guardian whom he knew would exercise an authority as judicious as his own. The two girls were remarkably handsome, and whenever they walked through the settlement, or drove abroad with their guardian, they attracted all the attention. Many a half-dusky heart was smitten of their white skin, which he would compare in colour to the pure snow that covers the plains. Now had the faces of the Red River beauties been Parian white, instead of dusky olive, the young *beaux* of the settlement would not have found their hearts beating half so wildly about the two pale daughters of the Hudson Bay Company's officer. They would indeed have languished for chestnut eyes, and complexions of Spain and the southern vineyards of France. But here amongst their sturdy "tiger blossoms," and passionate prairie roses blew two fair cold lilies; and their hearts bounded beyond measure at the thought of winning a look or a kindly smile. But the guardian watched the two pale girls closely, and permitted them to do little beyond his *surveillance*. There were not many whites in the circle of their acquaintance, but of this few, nearly every one was a suitor for one or other of the girls, yet for all the advances their hearts were still whole and they moved,

"In maiden meditation fancy free "

Now in Red River was a young half-breed, almost effeminate in manners, handsome in face and form, and agreeable and gentle in his address. He was indeed a sort of Bunthorne of the plains, just such a person as a romantic, shallow girl is most apt for a rose's period to sigh out her soul about. You find his type in fashionable civilised circles, in the languid dude who displays his dreams in his eyes to captivate the hearts of the silly girls, and— discreetly —keeps his mouth shut, to conceal his lack of brains. The two white daughters of the Company's officer were girls of ordinary understanding, but one of them had gotten too much poetry into her sweet head, and stood on the verge of a dizzy steep that overlooked a gulf, the name of which was Love. At a party given by one of the foremost of the half-breed families, this girl met Alexander, the Scottish half-breed, whose person and manners have been just described. There was something in the dreamy, far-away expression of the young Metis' eyes, which stirred the blood in the veins of the romantic girl. When they rested upon her, the soul of their owner seemed to yearn out to her. The voiceless, tender, passionate appealing in the look she was unable to forget when she walked along the grassy lanes, or trod the flower-rimmed path of the prairie.

Coming along in the hush of the summer evening, when only the lovemaking of the grasshoppers could be heard among the flowers, Alexander met her, He spoke no word, but there was the same tender, eloquent appealing in his eyes. He thought the young lady would not take it amiss of him, if he were to join her on her way over the fields; so he had taken the liberty.

There was a flutter at her heart, and a great passion-rose bloomed in each cheek.

No, she would not take it amiss. The walk was so pleasant! Indeed it was kind of him to join her.

The dusky lover spake few words; but he indolently left the path and gathered some sprays of wild flowers, and offered them to the girl. His eyes had the same, wistful look, and his brown fingers trembled as he offered the bouquet. Receiving them, and pinning them under her throat, she said in a low tone, while her voice trembled a little,

"When these fade, I shall press the petals in my book, and keep them always."

"Do you consider the flowers I gave you worth preserving?" he asked, his low voice likewise trembling.

"I do."

"I would give more than that," he said, tenderly, "to your keeping."

"Why," she enquired, with an unsuccessful attempt at displaying wonder, "what is it that you would give to my keeping?"

"My heart," the young man answered, his indolent eyes lighting up in the gloaming. She said nothing, but hung her head. The swarthy lover saw that she took no offence at his declaration. Indeed he gathered from the quivering of her red, moist lips, and from the tenderness in her eye, that the avowal had more than pleased her. She continued for a few seconds to look bashfully down at the path; and then she raised her eyes and looked at him. No more encouragement was needed.

"My beloved," he said, softly, and her head nestled upon his shoulder. There in the shadow of a small colony of poplars, on the verge of the boundless plain, shining under the full, ripe moon, each plighted troth to the other, and gave and received burning kisses. During the sweet, fast-fleeting hours on the calm plain, in her lover's arms, with no witness but the yellow moon, she took no heed of the barriers that lay between a union with her beloved; nor had he any foreboding of obstacles, but heard and declared vows of love, supremely happy.

Woman is a sort of Pandora's Box, the lid whereof is being forever raised, revealing the secrets within. The plighted maiden was flushed of cheek and unusually bright of eye when she returned to her home that evening. She could give her guardian no satisfactory account of her long absence, and told a very confused story about two paths, "you know," that were "very much alike"; but that "one led away around a poplar wood and out upon a portion of the prairie" which she did "not know." Here the sweet pet had got astray, and wandered around, although "it was so silly," till the sound of the bells of St. Boniface tolling ten had apprised her of the hour and also let her know where she was. Her guardian took the explanation, and contented himself with observing that he hoped it would be her last evening upon the prairie, straying around like an elk that had lost her mate.

"Jennie," said her sister, when they were alone, "you have not been telling the truth. You did not get astray on the prairie. Somebody has been courting you, and you are in love with him."

"I am in love; and it is true that some one has been courting me. I had intended to tell you all about it, my heart is so full. Now can you tell me who may my lover be?"

"I hope, Jennie," and the sister's eyes showed a blending of severity and sorrow, "that it is not Alexander."

"It is Alexander. Why should it not be? Is he not handsome, and gentle, and good? Wherefore then not he?"

"My God, do you know what such an alliance would cost you, would cost us all? Marriage with a half-breed would be a degradation; and a stain upon the whole family that never could be wiped out. O my poor unfortunate sister, ruin is what such a marriage would mean. Just that, my darling sister, and no less."

"I care not for that. I love him with all my heart and soul, and pledged myself to-night a hundred times to be his. I never can love another man; and he only shall possess me. What care I for the degradation of which you speak, as measured against the crowning misery, or the supreme happiness of my life? No; when Alexander is ready to say to me, Come, I shall go to him, and no threat nor persuasion shall dissuade me."

She spoke like all the heroic girls who afterwards meekly untie their bonnets just as they were ready to go to the church to wed against their keeper's will; and then sit down awaiting orders as to whom they must marry. Jennie was not the only girl who, in the first flush of passion, is prepared to go through fire, or die at the stake for the man she loves. Withal,—but that the proprieties forbid it—whenever young women make these dramatic declarations, the most appropriate course would be to give them a sound spanking, and put an end to the tragic business.

Nellie thought it her duty, and I suppose it was, to tell her bear-like guardian what had befallen to her sister. He was less disturbed on hearing the intelligence than Nellie supposed, and merely expressed some cold-blooded surprise at the presumption of the half-breed. He sat at his desk, and taking a sheet of paper, wrote this letter:

"To Alexander Saunders:

"DEAR SIR,—Would you be good enough to call at my house this evening at eight o'clock?

"Yours truly,

"Thomas Brown."

Having sealed and dispatched this note he resumed his work, without showing or feeling any further concern about the matter. When it was growing dark over the prairie that evening, the love-lorn Jennie saw her pleading-eyed lover pass along in the shadow of the poplars toward her guardian's house. She heard his ring at the door, and his step in the hall. Her heart was in a great flutter; but her sister was at her side giving her comfort. The doors were wide open, but everything was so husht, that the girls could plainly hear the following words spoken in the guardian's library:

"I understand, Mr. Saunders, that you have been taking the astonishingly presumptuous course of soliciting the hand of one of my wards. I am not given to severity, or I do not exactly know how I ought to resent an act which exhibits such a forgetfulness of what your attitude should be towards a person in the station of my ward. You are merely a half-breed; you are half-Indian, and for that matter might as well be Indian altogether. My ward's position is such that the bare idea of such a union is revolting. She is a lady by birth and by education, and is destined for a social sphere into which you could never, and ought never, enter. You may now go, sir, but you must remember that your ignorance is the only palliation of your presumption. Laurie, show this young man the way out."

"O, my God, what will become of me?" sobbed poor Jennie. "I cannot live! O, I will go after him! I will fly with him! I cannot endure this separation! O, sister, will you not intercede for my beloved? Tell uncle how noble and manly, and honourable he is! Can you not do anything for me? My God, what shall I do?"

In this fashion did poor Jennie's grief find words, and we leave her alone with her sore heart, while we follow the rejected suitor. He walked swiftly down the lawn, turning not his eye, or he might have seen in the window his lover, stretching imploring arms toward him. All his blood was running madly in his veins, and it burned like fire. His heart was hot, and his temples throbbed.

"So I am only a half-breed, and might as well be all Indian for that matter! O, God! A despised half-breed! They have shown the fangs at last. We now see how they regard us." And he went forth among his friends, and told the story of the insult and humiliation. A thousand half-breed hearts that night in Red River burned with vengeance against the white man; French Metis and English Metis alike had felt the sting of the indignity; and these two bodies, sundered before through petty cause, now united in a brotherhood of hate against the white population. It needs no further words to shew how ready these dusky people would be to rise and follow a crafty leader, who cried out:

"We are despised by these white people. We want no social or political alliance with them. We shall live apart, rather than in ignominy and union with them." Louis Riel was not ready the next morning to rise and lead the people to revolt, for this occurred some years before his bloody star reached the zenith; but the same hatred was there years later, when he turned the governor sent to the colony by the Dominion out of the territories, and set up an authority of his own. Well might the French historian, cognisant of the fate of the luckless suitor, and the consequences of the rejection, cry out with the poet:

> "*Amour tu perdis Troie.*" [Footnote: Love thou hast conquered even Troy.]

As for poor Jennie, heroic Jennie, who would follow her lover to death itself, she submitted, after a few sleepless nights, and days that for her were without a breakfast, to the mandate of the guardian, and to the philosophy of her sister. A little later, a tall, ungainly young Highlander came, offered himself, and took to his home the poetic and tragic daughter of the Company's officer.

Despite the blizzards that sometimes come sweeping across the prairie, smothering belated travellers, and un-roofing dwellings, notwithstanding the frequent incursions from regions in the far west of myriad-hosts of locusts and grasshoppers, Red River settlement throve in wealth and population, till, when the period with which I shall now deal arrived, it numbered no fewer than 15,000 souls. Upon the completion of the great Act of the Confederation of the British North American Provinces in 1867, the attention of Canadian statesmen was turned to this distant colony, and negotiations were opened for the transfer of the Territory to the Dominion. The back of great monopolies had now been broken. In 1858, England had resumed its great Indian empire and extinguished John Company; and this act had paved the way for a similar resumption of the vast prairie domain granted by King Charles to "the Governor and Company of Adventurers of England trading into Hudson Bay." The transfer was to be effected, as one writer puts it, by a triangular sort of arrangement. All territorial rights claimed by the Hudson Bay Company —and Red River lay within the Company's dominions—were to be annulled on payment of 300,000 pounds by Canada, and the country would then be handed over by Royal proclamation to the Dominion Government, the Company being allowed to retain only certain parcels of land in the vicinity of its trading posts. I may as well go upon the authority of the same writer. [Footnote: Captain G. L. Huyshe.] The transfer was dated for the 1st of December, 1869; but the Dominion Cabinet, eager to secure the rich prize, appointed its Minister of Public Works, the Honourable William McDougall, C.B., to be Lieutenant-Governor of the North-West Territories, and sent him off in the month of September, with instructions to proceed to Fort Garry "with all convenient speed" there to assist in the formal transfer of the Territories, and to "be ready to assume the Government" as soon as the transfer was completed. So far so well, but let us pause just here.

There is something to be said even on the side of revolt and murder, and let us see what it is. Since the foundation of the colony the people had lived under the government according to the laws propounded by the Hudson Bay Company. The people had established a civilization of their own, and had customs and rules which were always observed with great reverence. When tidings reached them that they were to be transferred to the Dominion of Canada, they began to have some misgivings as to how they should fare under the new order. Of late years, too, there had come into prominence among them a man whom early in these pages we saw bid good-bye to his father upon the plains on his way to school in the East. The fire seen in young Riel at the school, and when he turned his face again for the prairies that he loved, had now reached full flame. He had never ceased to impress upon the people that the Hudson Bay Company was a heartless, soulless corporation, and that the treatment accorded to the Metis was no better than might have been given to the dogs upon the plains.

There never was public peace after the tongue of this man had begun to make noise in the settlement.

When, therefore, it became known that the Canadian Government had determined upon taking the colony to itself, an ambitious scheme of the highest daring entered into the brain of Louis Riel. He lost no time in beginning to sow seeds of discontent.

"Canada," he said, "will absorb your colony, and as a people you will virtually be blotted out of existence. White officials will come here and lord it over you; the tax-gatherer will plunder the land for funds to build mighty docks, and canals, and bridges, and costly buildings, and numerous railroads in the East. The poor half-breed will be looked upon with contempt and curiosity: no custom that he regards as sacred will be respected; no right which is inherently his, will be acknowledged. They will send their own henchmen, who have no sympathy in common with the half-breeds, to rule over us; no complaint that the people make to the Central Government will be regarded; yea, this new rule will fasten itself upon us as some inexorable tyrant monster, driving deep its fangs into a soil that has been yours so long. Yes; you will be of *some* interest to them. You have some handsome wives and pretty daughters, and those virtuous pale-faces from the East have a strong admiration for lovely women. In this respect, you shall receive their attention."

The effect of such arguments among these credulous people, who saw not the wily traitor behind the rich, eloquent voice, quivering with indignation, was similar to that which would follow were you to fling a flaming torch upon the prairie in midsummer after a month of drought. Then the cunning deceiver went secretly to several of the leading half-breeds in Red River, and whispered certain proposals in their ear.

Meanwhile, events were transpiring which furnished just the very fuel that Riel wanted for his fire. During the summer of 1869, a surveying party, under Colonel Dennis, had been engaged surveying the country, and dividing it into townships, etc., for future allotment by government. According to good authority, the proceedings of this party had given great offence to the Metis. The unsettled state of the half-breeds' land tenure not unnaturally excited apprehension in the minds of these poor ignorant people that their lands would be taken from them, and given to Canadian immigrants. Then they had the burning words of Louis Riel ringing in their ears saying that the thing *would* be done. To lend colour to the mistrust, some members of the surveying party put up claims here and there to tracts of land to which they happened to take a fancy. But this was not all. Some of these gentlemen had the habit of giving the Indians drink till they became intoxicated, and then inducing them to make choice lands over to them. One could not pass through any superior tract of land without observing the stakes of some person or other of Colonel Dennis's party.

"I foretold it," cried Riel. "Go out for yourselves and see the marks they have set up bounding their plunder." Nor was this the only grievance presented to the half-breeds. The very survey then being carried on they looked upon as an act of contempt towards themselves; for Riel had put it in this light.

"The territory has not yet passed into the hands of the Canadian government"—and in saying this the Disturber was accurate—; "what right have they, therefore, to come here and lay down lines? It is as I have already told you: You are of as much importance in the eyes of the Canadian authorities, as would be so many dogs."

Nor were these the only grievances either. A "big man," a white, living at the settlement, had made himself obnoxious to the whole of Red River. He well knew how the people hated him, and he retorted by saying:

"Your scurvy race is almost run. Presently you will get into civilized hands, and be put through your facings. You disrespect me, but my counsels prevail at Ottawa. Only what I recommend, will the Government do; so that you see the settlement is very completely in my hands." This man was a valuable ally to Riel; for almost literally did he, while portending to speak for the Dominion authorities, corroborate the allegation of the arch agitator. Then two officials, Messrs Snow and Mair, sent out by Mr. McDougall, while he was yet Minister of Public Works, had established an intimacy with the obnoxious white man, received his hospitality, and given acquiescent ear to his advice. These two gentlemen looked upon the half-breeds as savages. They sent letters to the newspapers, describing Red River and its people in terms grossly unjust, and inaccurate. M. Riel got the communications and read them to the people.

"This," he said, "is the manner in which they describe our customs, our social life, and the virtue of our women." The women tossed their heads haughtily.

"We do what is right," they said, "and they can slander us if they will. We shall not prove, perhaps, so easy a prey to those white gallants as they seem to suppose." One high-spirited girl, and very beautiful, vowed that during the run of her life, she never would speak to a white man for this insult, or let him see her face. Yet, if the gossip is to be trusted, before the flowers bloomed thrice, after that, upon the prairie, she was sighing her sweet soul away, through her great gazelle eyes, for love of a sturdy young Englishman, who had taken up his abode upon the plains. And better than all the young fellow married her, and she is now one of the happiest, not to say one of the prettiest, women in Manitoba. Strong words of determination by a young woman are the most conclusive evidence that I know of the weakening of her resolve.

But Messrs Snow and Mair went on with their creditable work, and to their other good deeds it was alleged they added that of grabbing choice plots of land.

These two men were, of course, known to be the accredited agents of the Minister of Public Works; and Riel succeeded in convincing the credulous people that the Minister, indeed the whole government, were cognizant of their acts and approved of the same. "While public indignation was at its height, it was announced that a Lieutenant-Governor had been appointed for Red River, and that the man chosen was the very person through whom the chief indignity had been put upon the settlement. It was also shown with burning force by Riel that in a matter so important as the transfer of fifteen thousand people from one particular jurisdiction to another, they, the people transferred, had not been consulted. They had not, he also pointed out, been even formally apprised of the transfer.

"This Canadian Government take Red River and its half-breeds over, just as they would take over Red River and fifteen thousand sheep." And some of the men swore terrible oaths that this change should not be without resistance, and resistance to the death.

Riel said that the determination was good.

CHAPTER IV.

Having worked the unreasoning settlers to this pitch, Riel was satisfied. Public feeling needed but the fuse of some bold step of his to burst into instant flame. As the Lieutenant-Governor drew near the territory the agitator was almost beside himself with excitement. He neither ate nor slept but on foot or sleigh, was for ever moving from one to another perfecting plans, or inciting to tumult. At the house of a prominent half-breed, while the women sat about stitching, Riel met a number of the leading agitators, and thus addressed them:

"There are two courses open to us now. One is to continue as an unorganized band of noisy disturbers; the other, to league ourselves into an organized body for the defence and government of our country." This proposal thrilled the veins of his listeners, and pouting, coral-coloured female lips, said softly,

"Brava!"

A sort of fitful reflection followed the first wild burst of enthusiasm, and one *bois brule* arose and said:

"Far be it from me to utter one word that might dampen your ardor, but let us try to take some account of the cost. Would not such a step be an act of Rebellion? and is not Rebellion a treasonable offence?" At this point Riel, foaming with rage, arose and stopped him.

"We want no poltroonery, no alarmist sentiments here," he shouted. "Even though such an act were as you describe it, our duty as men, determined to guard their sacred rights, is to take the risk. But it would not be treason. The transfer of a people from one government to another is not constitutional without the people's consent. The Hudson's Bay Company have certain rights in the unsold lands of these regions; but no man, no corporation, no power, can sell, cede, or transfer that which is not his or its own property. Therefore the Hudson Bay Company has not the right to transfer our lands to the Dominion of Canada. And since we, the people of Red River, are not the chattels of the Company, they cannot transfer us. They have sold us to the Canadian government, but upon the ground between the two authorities will we stand, and create a province of our own. It may be that the Dominion Government will have justice enough to agree to this; if they oppose our rights, then I trust that there are men on Red River, who are not afraid to stand up for, yea to die for, their country." This speech was received with deafening acclamation.

At once a Provisional Government was formed, and at the instigation of Riel, John Bruce, who was a mere cat's-paw, was declared President. Riel himself took the Secretaryship; and very promptly the Secretary raised his voice.

"McDougall who sent his scourges here to plunder our land, and to ridicule our people, nears our border. There is no time to lose. *He must not enter.* I, therefore, move that the following letter be dispatched to him by a regularly constituted member of our Government:

"St. Nobert, Red River, October 21st, 1869.

"Sir,—The National Parliament of the Metis of Red River, hereby forbids you to enter the North-West Territories without a special permit from the National Government."

This motion was carried with enthusiasm. The letter was signed by the President and Secretary, and dispatched to Pembina, which was situate on the border, to await the arrival at that point of the Governor Designate. The pomp and daring of these proceedings had such an effect upon the colonists, that little by little they began to grow blind to the fact that their action was in the face of Canadian authority, and an invitation to a collision of arms. If anyone expressed any fear he was either savagely silenced by Riel, or informed that there were men enough in Red River to hold the country in the face of any force that could be sent against them. And the military enthusiasm of the Metis gave some colour to this latter assertion. An armed force, sufficient for present necessities, was established on Scratching River, a place about fifteen miles from Fort Garry. Here a barrier was put across the road by which McDougall must travel to reach Fort Garry, and beyond this the half-breeds swore the pale face Governor should never pass.

On the 30th day of October, Mr. McDougall arrived at Pembina. He was already aware that the country was seething with tumult; that Colonel Dennis had been turned out of the Territory; that Messrs. Snow & Mair had become hateful in the eyes of the half-breeds: yet he felt disposed to do little more than laugh at the whole affair. He had the assurance of his mischievous envoys that the matter was a mere temporary ebullition of feeling, and that his presence in the country would very soon calm the turbulent waters. So he said:

"I shall take no notice of this impertinent letter. In fact it is impossible for me to recognise such a piece of presumption, and deal with a communication which would be the rankest insolence, but that it is so extremely ludicrous." So the gallant Lieutenant-Governor, with his officials, boldly crossed the line and proceeded towards Fort Garry. But they were met on their triumphant march by a detachment of fourteen armed half-breeds whose spokesman said:

"You received an order from the Provisional Government not to enter these territories. When that order was passed it was the Government's intention to take care that it should be carried out. Yet you have forced yourself in here I give you till to-morrow morning to be clear of these territories." Mr. McDougall's lip began to hang a little low. The calm, even polite, tone of the spokesman of the party had impressed him more than bluster or rage. With the next morning came the same party. They made no noise, but quietly taking the horses of the Governor's party by the head, turned them around, and packed the whole of them back. In this way, and without so much as a loud word, was the Governor Designate turned out of the territories.

Every success, however trivial, was fuel to the courage and enthusiasm of Riel's party.

"I have begun this matter," the leader said to one of his followers, "and I do not mean to deal in half measures. Without stores we can do nothing. Fort Garry is worth our having just now, but we must move circumspectly in getting possession of it." So it was ordered that his followers should proceed in twos and threes, as if on no special mission, to the desired point. Presently, Governor McTavish saw in the shadow of the fort the rebel leader and a number of followers.

"We are desirous of entering," Riel said.

"Wherefore?" enquired the Governor.

"We cannot tell you now," was the reply; "it is enough for me to say that a great danger threatens the fort." Without further explanation, the feeble-willed Hudson Bay officer permitted the rebel and his followers to enter.

"Huzza!" they all shouted, when they found themselves inside the stockades, and glanced at tier upon tier of barrels of flour, and pork, and beef, and molasses; and upon the sacks of corn, and the warm clothing, and better than all, upon the arms and ammunition.

"I am at last master in Red River," Riel said to one of his followers. "My men can fight now, for here we have at once a fortification and a base of supplies."

Just a few words with reference to Mr. McDougall, and I shall dismiss him from these pages. He lived quietly at Pembina between the date of his expulsion from Red River and the first day of December. The latter date was fixed for the transfer of the new territory to the Dominion of Canada. So, towards midnight, on the 30th of November, the Governor-Designate and his party sallied, forth from the "line" and took formal possession of the territory in the name of the Government of Canada. There was no one stirring about the prairie on the night in question, for the glass shewed the thermometer to be 20 degrees below zero: so the gallant Governor was enabled to take possession without obstruction.

Riel was now fairly intoxicated with success. Some of his followers would sometimes ask him if he had no fear that the Canadian Government would send out a large force of soldiers against him. His invariable reply was:

"They never will do this. The way is too long, and the march too difficult. They will eventually make up their mind to let us rule this Province ourselves."

"And do you propose to stand aloof as an independent colony?"

"Perhaps! And, perhaps, we may, by and by, discuss the subject of annexation." For all the man's cunning and courage, he was almost as short-sighted as any savage upon the plain. And the small measure of Indian blood in him would assert itself in many ways. The people began to look upon him as another Napoleon triumphant, and to give him honour in every way that suggested itself. He made a great display of his importance, and would boast among his friends that he was as diplomatic and as able as any statesman in Canada, and that even his enemies admitted this. In his earlier days he sought, persistently, the smiles of the fair girls of the plains, but somehow or another he was never a very great favourite with the olive-skinned beauties. Now, however, the case was different with him. The Red River belles saw in him a hero and a statesman of the highest order, the ruler of a colony, and the defiant and triumphant enemy of the whole Dominion of Canada. So the poor, shallow pets began to ply their needles, and make for him presents of delicate things. One sewed gorgeous beads upon his hunting coat, and another set his jacket spangling with quills of the porcupine. The good priests of Red River, and their pious vicar, *pere* Lestanc, whom Monseigneur had left in charge of the Diocese while he was attending the Ecumenical Council in Rome, came forward with their homage. These worthy gentlemen had been in the habit of reading from the Catechism ever since the time they were first able to tell their beads, or to make mud pies, these words: "He that resisteth the power, resisteth the ordinance of God; and they that (so) resist shall purchase to themselves damnation." Here was a madly ambitious adventurer "resisting the power," and, therefore, "resisting the ordinances of God;" but these precious divines saw no harm whatever in the act. Indeed, they were the most persistent abettors in the uprising, counselling their flock to be zealous and firm, and to follow the advice of their patriotic and able leader, M. Riel. The great swaggering, windy *pere* Richot, took his coarse person from house to house denouncing the Canadian Government and inciting the people.

"No harm can come to you," he would say; "you have in the Canadian Government a good friend in Mr. George E. Cartier. He will see that no hair of one of your heads is touched." And Riel went abroad giving the same assurance. Moreover, it was known to every thinking one of the fifteen thousand Metis that Riel was a *protege* of Monseigneur Tache; that through this pious bishop it was he had received his education, and that His Lordship would not alone seek to minimize what his favourite had done, but would say that the uprising was a justifiable one. This was how the Catholic Church in Red River stimulated the diseased vanity and the lawless spirit of this thrice-dangerous Guiteau of the plains.

I have already said that Bruce was put up by Riel as a mere figure-head. When the end of the pretence had been accomplished, this poor scare-crow was thrown down and Louis Riel assumed the presidency of the Provisional Government. Now he began to draw to himself all those men whom he knew would be faithful tools in carrying out any scheme of villainy, or even of blood that he proposed to them. The coarse and loud-mouthed O'Donoghue was duly installed as a confidential attendant with wide powers, and Lepine was made head of the military part of the insurrectionary body. It certainly was strange if the treasonable undertaking should not be successful with the acquisition of all the fearless and lawless personages that the half-breed community could produce, and the vicar-general and the swaggering father Richot offering up masses that it should prevail.

It must not be supposed that there were no white people in this Red River region. There were very many indeed, and some of them held prominent places in the community through high character or through affluence. Most of these persons were loyal to the heart's core, and were of opinion that the rising had nothing justifiable in it, and regarded it as a criminal and treasonable rebellion. At meetings, held in the town of Winnipeg, some of these gentlemen were at no pains to give expression to their sentiments. But Riel's murderous eye was upon them; and he was revolving over divers plans of vengeance. There was no reason why he should hesitate in taking any step that promised help to the cause, for Holy Church was praying for its success, and working for it, too. The shedding of the blood of a few heretics was a matter of small consequence: indeed, the act would only hallow a cause that had patriotism under, and religion behind it. We shall leave Riel glaring with wolfish eyes upon the good men who raised their voices against lawlessness, and relate a story which will shed a new light upon the darkest deed of the dark career of the miscreant Rebel.

CHAPTER V.

Some time before the outbreak, Riel, in company with a half-breed, had gone in the autumn shooting chicken along the prairies. The hunting-ground was many miles distant from Riel's home, so that the intention of the sportsmen was to trust themselves to the hospitality of some farm-house in the neighbourhood. The settlers were all, with two or three exceptions, Metis; and the door of the half-breed is never shut against traveller or stranger. One late afternoon, as the two men were passing along the prairie footpath towards a little settlement, they heard at some distance over the plain, a girl singing. The song was exquisitely worded and touching, and the singer's voice was sweet and limpid as the notes of a bobolink. M. Riel, like Mohammed, El Mahdi, and other great patrons of race and religion, is strong of will; but he is weaker than a shorn Samson when a lovely woman chooses to essay a conquest. So he marvelled much to his companion as to who the singer might be, and proposed that both should leave the path and join the unknown fair one. A few minutes walk brought the two beyond a small poplar grove, and there, upon a fallen tree-bole, in the delicious cool of the autumn evening, they saw the songstress sitting. She was a maiden of about eighteen years, and her soft, silky-fine, dark hair was over her shoulders. In girlish fancy she had woven for herself a crown of flowers out of marigolds and daisies, and put it upon her head. She did not hear the footsteps of the men upon the soft prairie, and they did not at once reveal themselves, but stood a little way back listening to her. She had ceased her song, and was gazing beyond intently. On the naked limb of a desolate, thunder-riven tree that stood apart from its lush, green-boughed neighbours, sat a lonely thrush in seeming melancholy. Every few seconds he would utter a note of song. Sometimes it was low and sorrowful, then it was louder, with the same sad quality in it, as if the lonely bird were calling for some responsive voice from far away over the prairie.

"Dear bird, you have lost your mate, and are crying out for her," the girl said, stretching out her little brown hand compassionately toward the low-crouching songster. "Your companions have gone to the South, and you wait here trusting that your mate will come back, and not journey to summer lands without you. Is not that so, my poor bird? Ah, would that I could go with you where there are always flowers, and ever can be heard the ripple of little brooks. Here the leaves will soon fall, ah, me! and the daisies wither, and instead of the delight of summer we shall have only the cry of hungry wolves, and the bellowing of bitter winds above the ghastly plains. But could I go to the South, there is no one who would sing over my absence one lamenting note, as you sing, my bird, for the mate with whom you had so many hours of sweet lovemaking in these prairie thickets. Nobody loves me woos me, cares for me, or sings about me. I am not even as the wild rose here, though it seems to be alone and is forbidden to take its walk: for it holds up its bright face and can see its lover; and he breathes back upon the kind, willing, breeze-puffs, through all the summer, sweet-scented love messages, tidings of a matrimony as delicious as that of the angels." She stood up, and raised her arms above her head yearningly. The autumn wind was cooing in her hair, and softly swaying its silken meshes.

"Fare well, my desolate one: may your poor little heart be gladder soon. Could I but be a bird, arid you would have me for a companion, your lamenting should not be for long. We should journey loitering and love-making all the long sweet way, from here to the South, and have no repining."

Turning around, she perceived two men standing close beside her. She became very confused, and clutched for the blanket to cover her face, but she had strayed away among the flowers without it. Very deeply she blushed that the strangers should have heard her; and she spake not.

"Bon jour, ma belle fille." It was M. Riel who had addressed her. He drew closer, and she, in a very low voice, her olive face stained with a faint flush of crimson, answered,

"Bon jour, Monsieur."

"Be not abashed. We heard what you were saying to the bird, and I think the sentiments were very pretty."

This but confused the little prairie beauty all the more. But the gallant stranger took no heed of her embarrassment.

"With part of your declaration I cannot agree. A maiden with such charms as yours is not left long to sigh for a lover. Believe me, I should like to be that bird to whom you said you would, if you could, offer love and companionship." M. Riel made no disguise of his admiration for the beautiful girl of the plains. He stepped up by her side and was about to take her hand after delivering himself of this gallant speech, but she quickly drew it away. Passing through a covert as they neared the little settlement, Riel's sportsman companion walked ahead, leaving the other two some distance in the rear. The ravishing beauty of the girl was more than the amorously-disposed stranger could resist, and suddenly throwing his arms around her he sought to kiss her. But the soft-eyed fawn of the desert soon showed herself in the guise of a petit bete sauvage. With a startling scream she bounded away from his grasp.

"How do you dare take this liberty with me, Monsieur," she said, her eyes kindled with anger and wounded pride. "You first meanly come and intrude upon my privacy; next you must turn what knowledge you gain by acting spy and eavesdropper, into a means of offering me insult. You have heard me say that I had no lover to sigh for me. I spoke the truth: I *have* no such lover. But you I will not accept as one; your very sight is already hateful to me." And turning, with flushed cheek and gleaming eyes, she entered the cosy, cleanly-kept little cottage of her father. But she soon reflected that she had been guilty of an unpardonably inhospitable act in not asking the strangers to enter. Suddenly turning, she walked rapidly back, and overtook the crest-fallen wooer and his companion, and said in a voice from which every trace of her late anger had disappeared.

"Entrez, Messieurs."

M. Riel's countenance speedily lost its gloom, and, respectfully touching his hat, he said:

"Oui, Mademoiselle, avec le plus grand plaisir." Tripping lightly ahead she announced the two strangers, and then returned, going to the bars where the cows were lowing, waiting to be milked. The persistent sportsman had not by any means made up his mind to desist in the wooing.

"The colt shies," he murmured, "when she first sees the halter. Presently she becomes tractable enough." Then, while he sat waiting for the evening meal, blithely through the hush of the exquisite evening came the voice of the girl. She was singing from *La Claire Fontaine*:

  "A la claire fontaine
  Je m'allait promener,
  J'ai trouve l'eau si belle
  Que je me suis baigne."

Her song ended with her work, and as she passed the strangers, with her two flowing pails of yellow milk, Riel whispered softly, as he touched her sweet little hand.

"Ah, ma petite amie!"

The same flash came in her eyes, the same proud blood mantled through the dusk of her cheek, but she restrained herself. He was a guest under her father's roof, and she would suffer the offence to pass. The persistent gallant was more crest-fallen by this last silent rebuke, than by the first with its angry words. The first, in his vanity, he had deemed an outburst of petulance, instead of an expression of personal dislike, especially as the girl had so suddenly calmed herself and extended hospitalities. He gnashed his teeth that a half-breed girl, in an obscure village, should resent his advances;

he for whom, if his own understanding was to be trusted, so many bright eyes were languishing. At the evening meal he received courteous, kindly attention from Marie; but this was all. He related with much eloquence all that he had seen in the big world in the East during his school days, and took good care that his hosts should know how important a person he was in the colony of Red River. To his mortification he frequently observed in the midst of one of his most self-glorifying speeches that the girl's eyes were abstracted, as if her imagination were wandering. He was certain she was not interested in him, or in his exploits.

"Can she have a lover?" he asked himself, a keen arrow of jealousy entering at his heart, and vibrating through all his veins. "No, this cannot be. She said in her musings on the prairie that she had nobody who would sing a sad song if she were to go to the South. Stop! She may love, and not find her passion requited. I shall stay about here some days, upon some pretext, and I shall see what is in the wind."

The next morning, when breakfast was ended, he perceived Marie rush to the window, and then hastily, and with a dainty coyness withdraw her head from the pane. Simultaneously he heard a sprightly tune whistled, as if by some glad, young heart that knew no care. Looking now, he saw a tall, well-formed young whiteman, a gun on his back, and a dog at his heels, walking along the little meadow-path toward the cottage.

"This is the lover," he muttered; "curses upon him." From that moment he hated with all the bitterness of his nature the man now striding carelessly up toward the cottage door.

"Bon jour, mademoiselle et messieurs" the newcomer said in cheery tones, as he entered, making a low bow.

"Bon jour, Monsieur Scott," was the reply. Louis Riel, intently watching, saw the girl's colour come and go as she spoke to the young man. This was the same Scott, the Thomas Scott, the tidings of whose fate, at the hands of the rebel and murderer, Louis Riel, in later years, sent the blood boiling through the veins of Western Canada. The young man stayed only for a few moments, and Riel observed that everybody in the house treated him as if in some way he had been the benefactor of all. When he arose to go, young Jean, who knew of every widgeon in the mere beyond the cottonwood grove, and where the last flock of quail had been seen to alight, followed him out the door, and very secretly communicated his knowledge. Marie had seen a large flock of turkeys upon the prairie a few moments walk south of the poplar grove, and perhaps they had not yet gone away.

"When did you see them, ma chere mademoiselle Marie? enquired Scott. You know turkeys do not settle down like immigrants in one spot, and wait till we inhabitants of the plains come out and shoot them. Was it last week, or only the day before yesterday that you saw them?" There was a very merry twinkle in his eye as he went on with this banter. Marie affected to pout, but she answered.

"This morning, while the dew was shining upon the grass, and you, I doubt not, were sleeping soundly, I was abroad on the plains for the cows. It was then I saw them. I am glad, however, that you have pointed out the difference between turkeys and immigrants. I did not know it before." He handed her a tiger lily which he had plucked on the way, saying,

"There, for your valuable information, I give you that. Next time I come, if you are able to tell me where I can find several flocks, I shall bring you some coppers." With a world of mischief in his eyes, he disappeared, and Mary, in spite of herself, could not conceal from everybody in the house a quick little sigh at his departure.

"It seems to me this Monsieur Scott is a great favourite with your folk, Monsieur?" Said M. Riel, when the young man had left the cottage. "Now I came with my friend also for sport, but no pretty eyes had seen any flocks to reserve for me." And he gave a somewhat sneering glance at poor Marie, who was pretending to be engaged in examining the petals of the tiger-lilly, although she was all the while thinking of the mischievous, manly, sunny-hearted lad who had given it to her. M. Riel's words and the sneer were lost, so far as she was concerned. Her ears were where her heart was, out on the plain beyond the cottonwood, where she could see the tall, straight, lithe figure of young Scott, with his dog at his heels, its head now bobbing up from the grass, and now its tail.

"Oui, Monsieur," returned Marie's father, "Monsieur Scott is a very great favourite with our family. We are under an obligation to him that it will be difficult for us ever to repay."

"Whence comes this benefactor," queried M. Riel, with an ugly sneer, "and how has he placed you under such obligation?" Then, reflecting that he was showing a bitterness respecting the young man which he could just then neither explain nor justify, he said:

"Mais, pardonnez moi. Think me not rude for asking these questions. When pretty eyes are employed to see, and pretty lips to tell of, game for one sportsman in preference to another, the neglected one may be excused for seeking to know in what way fortune has been kind with his rival."

"Shall I tell the whole story, Marie?" enquired the *pere*, "or will you do so?"

"O I know that you will not leave anything out that can show, the bravery of Mr. Scott, so I shall leave you to tell it," replied the girl.

"Well, last spring, Marie was spending some days with her aunt, a few miles up Red River. It was the flood time, and as you remember the river was swollen to a point higher than it had ever reached within the memory of any body in the settlement. Marie is venturesome, and since a child has shown a keen delight in going upon boats, or paddling a canoe; so one day, during the visit which I have mentioned, she got into a birch that swung in a little pond formed behind her uncle's premises by the over-flowing of the stream's channel. Untying the canoe, she seized the blade and began to paddle about in the lazy water. Presently she reached the eddies, which, since a child, she has always called the 'rings of the water-witches,' wherever she learned that term. Her cousin, Violette, was standing in the doorway, as she saw Marie move off, and she cried out to her to beware of the eddies; but my daughter, wayward and reckless, as it is her habit to be in such matters, merely replied with a laugh; and then, as the canoe began to turn round and round in the gurgling circles, she cried out, 'I am in the rings of the water-witches. C'est bon! bon! C'est magnifique! O I wish you were with me, Violette, ma chere. It is so delightful to go round and round.' A little way beyond, not more than twice the canoe's length, rushed by, roaring, the full tide of the river. 'Beware, Marie, beware, for the love of heaven, of the river. If you get a little further out, and these eddies will drag you out, you will be in the mad current, and no arm can paddle the canoe to land out of the flood. Then, dear, there is the fall below, and the fans of the mill. Come back, won't you!' But my daughter heeded not the words. She only laughed, and began dipping water up from the eddies with the paddle-blade, as if it were a spoon that she held in her hand. 'I am dipping water from the witches rings,' she cried. 'How the drops sparkle! Every one is a glittering jewel of priceless value. I wish you were here with me, Violette!' Suddenly, and in an altered tone, she cried, 'Mon Dieu! My paddle is gone.' The paddle had no sooner glided out into the rushing, turbulent waters than the canoe followed it, and Marie saw herself drifting on to her doom. Half a mile below was the fall, and at the side of the fall, went ever and ever around with tremendous violence, the rending fans of the water-mill. Marie knew full well that any drift boat, or log, or raft, carried down the river at freshet-flow, was always swept into the toils of the inexorable wheels. Yet, if she were reckless and without heed a few minutes before, I am told that now she was calm. As she is present, I must refrain from too much eulogy of her behaviour. Violette gave the alarm that Marie was adrift in the river without a paddle, and in a few seconds, every body living near had turned out, and were running down the shore. Several brought paddles, but it took hard running to keep up with the canoe, for the flood was racing at a speed of eight miles an hour. When they did get up in line each one flung out a paddle. But one fell too far out, and another not far enough. About fifteen men were about the banks in violent excitement, and every one of them saw nothing but doom for Marie. As the canoe neared a point about two hundred yards above the fall, a young white man—all the rest were bois-brules—rushed out upon the bank, with a paddle in his hand, and, without a word, leaped into the mad waters. With a few strokes, he was at the side of the canoe, and put the paddle into Marie's hand. 'Here,' he said, 'Keep away from the mill; that is your only danger, and steer sheer over the fall, getting as close as possible to the left bank.' The height of the fall, as you are aware, was not more than fifteen or eighteen feet, and there was plenty of water below, and not very much danger from rocks. 'Go you on shore now, and I will meet my doom, or achieve my safety,' Marie said; but the young man answered, 'Nay, I will go over the fall too: I can then be of some service to you.' So he swam along by the canoe's side directing my daughter, and shaping the course of the prow on the very brink of the fall. Then all shot over together. The canoe and Marie, and the young man were buried far under the terrible mass of water, but they soon came to the surface again, when the heroic stranger saved my daughter, and through the fury of the mad churning waters, landed her safe and unhurt upon the bank. The young man was Thomas Scott, whom you saw here this morning. Is it any wonder, think you, that when Marie sees wild turkeys upon the prairie, she keeps the knowledge of it to herself till she gets the ear of her deliverer? Think you, now, that it is strange he should be looked upon by us as a benefactor?"

"A very brave act, indeed, on the part of this young man," replied the swarthy M. Riel. "He has excellent judgment, I perceive, or he would not so readily have calculated that no harm could come to any one who could swim well by being carried over the falls."

Marie's eyes flashed indignantly at this cold blooded discounting of the generous, uncalculating bravery of her young preserver.

"I doubt, Monsieur, she said, whether if you had been on the bank where Monsieur Scott jumped in, you would have looked upon the going over of the fall as an exploit so free of danger as you describe it now. As a matter of fact, there *were* many half-breeds there, many of whom, no doubt, were as brave as yourself, but I should have perished in the fans of the mill if I had to depend upon the succour of any one of them."

"Mademoiselle," he retorted with a fierce light in his eye, "I am not a half-breed."

"O, pardonnez mois, I thought from your features and the straightness of your coal-black hair, that you were." Riel's blood was nigh unto boiling in his veins, but he had craft enough to preserve a tolerably unruffled exterior.

"And in return for this great bravery, ma petite demoiselle has, I suppose, given her heart to her deliverer?"

"I think Monsieur is impertinent; and I shall ask my father to forbid him to continue to address me in such a manner."

"A thousand pardons; I did not mean to pain, but only to chaff, your brave daughter. I think that Monsieur Scott is most fortunate in having a friend, a beautiful friend, so loyal to him, and so jealous of his fair fame. But to pass to other matters. Have you had visits from any emissaries of the Canadian government during the autumn?"

"Yes, Monsieur Mair came here one day in company with Monsieur Scott. They were both quail shooting. They stayed only for a little, and I was quite favourably impressed with the agreeableness and politeness of M. Mair's manners."

"O, indeed! Monsieur Mair was here and with Mr. Scott! I am glad that you conceive an opinion so favourable of Monsieur Mair, but I regret that I am unable to share in the regard. I think I had better open your eyes somewhat to the character of this agreeable gentleman. Since coming to Red River, his chief occupation has been writing correspondence respecting our colony, and the civilization and morals of our people. I have been preserving carefully some of the communications for future use, and if you will permit me I shall read an extract from a late contribution of his to a newspaper printed in Ontario. You will, I think, be able to gather from it something of his opinion respecting the Metis women. Indeed, I am surprised that Mademoiselle's great friend and preserver," he looked sneeringly at Marie, "should have for so close a companion a person who entertains these views about our people."

"I do not know that Monsieur Scott is so close a companion of Monsieur Mair," put in Marie. "I think Monsieur is now, as he has been doing all along, assuming quite too much."

"I sincerely trust that I am doing so, but I shall read the extract," and he took from his pocket-book a newspaper slip. Smoothing the creases out of the same, he read, with the most malignant glee, the following paragraph, dwelling with emphasis upon every disparaging epithet:—

> "Here I am in Red River settlement. What a paradise of a place it is. The mud, which is a beautiful dusky red, like the complexion of the Red River belles, does not rise much beyond my knees; and resembling the brown-skinned beauties in more than complexion, it affectionately clings to me, and do what I will, I cannot get rid of it."

"That is a very flattering description of our Red River young women, I am sure, and from the pen of your great friend's friend, too. Now is it not? But there is more than this," and he proceeded to read further.

> "The other evening they had a pow-wow in the settlement, which they called a dance. I was invited, and being considered such a great man here, of course—I do not speak it boastingly—the hearts of all the tallow-complexioned girls throbbed at a great rate when I entered."

"Tallow complexioned girls!" reiterated the reader. "Very complimentary, indeed, on the part of the friend of your greatest friend."

"Monsieur will either please finish reading his slip, since he wishes to do so, although, for my part, I am not at all interested in it, or put it by. In any case, I must ask that he will cease addressing me in this insolent tone."

"Then, since Mademoiselle wills it so, I shall finish the very truthful and complimentary paragraph without further comment."

> "Such a bear garden as that dance was; yet I somewhat enjoyed the languishing glances of the bright-eyed damsels. But, ugh! the savages never can be made to wash themselves. When the dance had continued for three or four hours, the dancers began to pair off like pigeons and in each nook you could observe a half-breed and his girl, sometimes the demoiselle nursing her beau with arms about his neck, or *vice versa*. ... The women are all slatterns, and as a rule they exhibit about as much morality as is found among the female elk of the prairies. A white man here who is at all successful in winning female attention, needs but to whistle, or to raise his finger, to have half a dozen of the dusky beauties running after him. While I write this letter I see two maidens passing under my window. I no longer take pride or fun in the matter. To me they have become a nuisance."

CHAPTER VI.

"Now, Monsieur," said M. Riel, folding his newspaper slip and putting it back again into his greasy pocket-book, "you well perceive that this Monsieur Mair is not exactly the sort of gentleman who ought to be the recipient of your hospitalities. I do not say that Monsieur Scott, who went over the little waterfall with your daughter, holds the same opinion respecting us, as as does his friend Monsieur Mair; I only know that upon matters of this kind bosom friends are very apt to be of the same mind.

"Who, let me ask again, has informed the gallant and generous Monsieur that these two young white men are bosom friends? Monsieur Mair was at this house once, and Monsieur Scott was with him. I understood that they had only met the day before; and it is only a week ago since Monsieur told me that he had not since seen his new friend. Monsieur has been sarcastic in his reference to Monsieur Scott, I think without much excuse."

"Is not this, Monsieur Scott, an employe of the Vampire Snow, who is making surveys through our territories in our despite, and in the face of law and justice?" Marie's father replied:

"Il est, Monsieur."

"So I had been informed. Now Monsieur, I have some serious business to talk to you about. As you are no doubt aware, the authorities at the Canadian Capital are at this moment discussing the project of buying the North-West Territories from the Hudson Bay Company, converting Red River into a Dominion Colony of the Confederation, and setting to rule it a governor and officials chosen from among Canadians, who hold opinions respecting us as a people, quite similar to those entertained by Monsieur Mair, and those who have the honour of being his friend." This with a malignant glance toward Marie, who merely retorted with a scornful flash in her fine, proud eyes.

"Well, Monsieur, I have decided that Red River shall not pass over to the hands of alien officials. I shall call upon every true colonist to rise and aid me in asserting our rights as free men, and as the proprietors of the soil we have tilled for so many years. As for your friend Mr. Scott, Mademoiselle"—turning with a hideous look toward Marie—"I am very sorry to interfere with his good fortune, but before the set of to-morrow's sun, I intend packing Mr. Snow and his followers out of our territories. Nay more, I shall keep a very sharp look out for this young man who went with you over the chute petite. Indeed it may be interesting for you to hear that I know something of his antecedents already. He delights to call himself a 'loyalist,' and has declared that the people of Red River have no right to protest against the transfer to the Canadian Government."

"I do not know what Monsieur Scott's views are upon this question," replied the girl. "Whatever they are I presume that he is as much entitled to hold them as you are to maintain yours."

"I am not so certain on this point as ma belle Mademoiselle seems to be," he retorted with a sneer like the hiss of a cobra. "This is our country, and any man who opposes its welfare is a traitor and a common enemy. But now, Monsieur,"—turning to Marie's father—"you must permit me to say that I view with strong disapproval the intimacy of any of our people with aliens and enemies. Therefore I find it necessary to forbid for the future any further visit of this young man Scott to your house. Nay, more, I shall not permit any communication between your family and him; as I have good reason to believe that he is a paid spy of Mr. Snow and the Government of Canada."

"Monsieur," quietly retorted Marie, with a curl of infinite contempt upon her soft, red-ripe, moist lips, "You are a coward, and a snake."

"Hush, Marie! Monsieur must not take heed of the ready tongue of my daughter," the poor terrified and over-credulous father put in with much trepidation.

"Mon pere need not apologize to Monsieur Riel for sa fille," the girl said, giving her father a glance of mild reproach. "I think that I am not unaware of the reason why Monsieur Riel's patriotism and vigilance have taken their present generous, honourable and manly form. And as I have now to go out and attend to my work, I would desire to say before leaving, that Monsieur has addressed his last words to me. I do not wish to see him ever again at our house. Should he insist on coming—and I know he has high spirit and honourable feeling enough to even so insist and force himself where he is not welcome—it shall be to my greatest repugnance. I have been to you, mon pere, a faithful and loving child. I do not think that I have ever before this day made any important request of you. But I make one now: it is that you request this Monsieur Riel to never enter our doors again. Pray, mon pere," she said going to him and looking into his face with the intensest pleading in her great eyes, "do not refuse me this request."

"Monsieur has heard my daughter's request? I cannot deny it to her."

The only reply from M. Riel was a sneer that sounded like an envenomed hiss.

"About the matter of visits, Monsieur, I shall consult my own taste and convenience." Marie went out from the house as regal in her bearing, and as beautiful as any princess that has ever trod the court of Caliph. Riel followed the retreating form of the lovely girl with eyes that showed the rage and desire of a wild beast. When she was out of sight he calmed himself, and assuming a changed mood, turned to her father.

"Monsieur, there is no reason why you and I should quarrel; is there?"

"No Monsieur; no reason."

"On the contrary, it would be well, if in these troublous times, when duties so momentous await every loyal heart in the colony, that we should be friends. Is this not so?"

"Oui, Monsieur."

"Then we can, if you will, be friends. I am prepared to forgive the indignity put upon, me by your daughter. I will not hesitate to take your hand, and forgive you for the insult which you have just offered me. And now hear what I have to say. Coming yonder through the prairie, yesterday, I heard your daughter singing. The very sound of her voice thrilled me as I had never been delighted in all my life before. But when I saw her, sitting alone, a d heard her holding converse with a solitary bird which had lost its mate, I was ravished by her beauty, and made a vow that I would win her heart. I presently perceived that the impression I made upon her was not favourable. I took her hand in mine, but she snatched it away as if an aspek's tongue had touched it. A moment later, in the madness of my passion for her, I suddenly strained her in my arms. After this I knew that she detested me. This knowledge I could have borne, trusting to time, and to the aid of fortune, to make her look less indifferently upon me. Great achievement lies almost ready at my hand; and my end attained, she would have seen in me one who stood above all others in Red River in brilliancy of attainment and strength of character. And while in this way I was endeavouring to cool the fire that was burning me, I perceived that her heart was given to another; to one who, so far as I can judge, does not return her affection."

"And who, pray Monsieur, may this rival be?"

"The young man who rescued your daughter—Thomas Scott."

"Mon Dieu, I hope that it is not as you say, for I do not want my daughter, much as I am indebted to this young man, to give to him her affection. If he be, as you say, a spy of Government and an enemy of our people, a marriage with him would be out of the question."

"Bon, bon! Monsieur." And M. Riel, in the exuberance of his loyalty, having succeeded in the vital point, grasped the hand of Marie's father and shook and wrung it several times.

"Now, Monsieur, we agree on the main point. I shall name the other conditions upon which we may be friends. I have sworn to overcome your daughter's repugnance to me. Will you assist me in the direction of accomplishing this object?"

"Oui, Monsieur, by every *fair* means."

"C'est bien. By every fair means. Only fair means will I ask you to employ. I shall now tell you what I desire you to do. You must keep Mademoiselle under your strictest surveillance. She must not see Monsieur Scott, or communicate with him. When his name is introduced into conversation, you must show that the subject is displeasing to you. You will be asked why it is so, and you shall answer that you have indisputable proof, and such proof you may take my *word* to be, that the young man is not in sympathy with the cause of the Metis, and that he is actually a secret and paid agent of the Canadian Government. That your course may seem more reasonable, and appear to be the outcome of your own inclination, you will on such occasions be able to say that you are under obligation to him for his readiness and gallantry—always use these words—when your daughter was in the brimming river; but that your gratitude can be only a, memory, since he has leagued himself against a cause so near to the heart, and so supremely in the interest, of every man and woman and child in the colony of Red River. You must at the very first convenient moment, and without letting Marie perceive that I have prompted you to this step, inform her that she must banish from her mind at once any tender fancies regarding the young man which she may possess. Point out to her that in any case it would be unwise in her to cherish feelings which very evidently are not reciprocated. Lastly, you will have to teach her cautiously, and without the semblance of coercion, but constantly, to think of me. You must show her how great is the promise which lies before me; how I am the leader of the people and ruler-predestined of all the land. Nor must you forget to show her that if I have seemed rude in her presence, and given way to anger or bitterness, it was because of my all-consuming love for her, and that henceforth the great aim of my life, through all the turbulent deeds that this tumultous time may have in store for me, shall be to win her approbation, to hear at the close of the din, and when achievement shall have crowned me master, a 'Brava, Monsieur' from her sweet lips.'

"Most faithfully, Monsieur, I swear to you," answered the old man, taking the Rebel's hand in his, "will your wishes be carried out. More than this, I can almost promise you that I shall succeed." And then he went to fetch a bottle, in which he had some choice old rye. While he was away, M. Riel, who was alone—for all were absent in the fields, and his comrade had been abroad since the grey dawn—began to muse in this wise:

"So he believes that he can triumph—that Marie will yield!" Then he ground his teeth like a wild beast and swore a terrible oath. "If she yield—ah! but it is a feast for me to contemplate my revenge. Raise her to the dignity of wife to share my social honours and triumph. No; elle sera ma maitresse; and I shall cast her off among the worthless and degraded ones of her sex." Then Marie's father entered with the liquor, and pledged his fealty to Monsieur with many "salutes" and "bonne santes" After M. Riel had taken sufficient liquor to make him thoroughly daring, he said with a sinister tone:

"Although it may not be your honour ever to call me your son-in-law, your duty in persuading your daughter remains the same. We have formed a compact of friendship and mutual understanding; yet I must say to you that your own personal safety depends upon your compliance; depends" he repeated, raising his voice till it sounded like the bellowing of an infuriated bull, "*upon your success*. Your intimacy with this man Scott, together with the visit paid to your house by the man Mair, places you entirely at my mercy. Before many days I shall call again to see how far you have succeeded. I shall expect a report of some progress. When I call after that I shall be satisfied with nothing short of *triumph*. I now go, leaving my warning to ring in your ears till you see me again." And with an air of insolent mastery, and a gross light in his eye, he seized his fowling-piece, and strode out the door, followed by his dog.

"Mon Dieu!" gasped the terrified half-breed, "I thought that we had become friends, but he goes from my door like an enemy, filling my ears with threats of vengeance. May the Virgin protect my Marie and me from his power."

"Has that terrible man gone, mon pere?" enquired Marie, who now entered with sorrow and agitation in her face.

"Yes; but you must not speak against him. O, how I fear him; that is to say, ma petite fille, he is a very powerful man, a great man, and will one day rule all the people, and be in eminence like unto one of the Canadian Governors: therefore, it is that it was unfortunate the young man Scott should ever have been at our house."

"Ah, mon pere! wherefore? Do you regret having extended a trifling hospitality, not better than you would accord to a wandering savage, to a brave, honest, honourable young man, who, at the risk, of his own life, saved the life of your child? O, surely you have not received into your ears the poison of this man's cunning and malice;" and she threw her arms about her father's neck and sobbed, and sobbed there as if her heart would burst. Old Jean was moved to deep grief at the affliction of his daughter, yet he could offer her no word of comfort.

"Monsieur has poured no poison into my ear, ma chere. He is a powerful man and a great patriot. The people all love him; and, although he spoke rudely and bitterly to you, we must forgive him. This we shall not find difficult to do, when we remember that his display of ill-feeling was because of his all-consuming love for you."

"All-consuming *love!*" and her eyes blazed with indignation. "All-consuming, all debasing, low passion; not love. No, no; love is a sacred thing, whose divine name is polluted when uttered by such lips as his."

"Be reasonable, ma Marie; don't suffer hastily formed dislikes to sway your judgment and good sense. There is not a girl on all the prairies who would not be proud to be wooed by Monsieur Riel. Wherefore should you not be? If you have any other affection in your heart banish it. It may be that you have cherished a tender regard for the young man Scott, who is, let me see what he is, who is ready and gallant—no, that is not it—who is quick, and brave, yes, I think that is it———."

"Mon Dieu; cease, mon pere. Has this tempter gone so far as to actually put in your mouth the words to be employed in winning me to his hateful, loathsome arms. Mon Dieu, Mon Dieu;" and she pressed her little brown fingers over her throbbing temples. Has my own father leagued himself against my happiness and, and—my *honour!*" And, with a loud, heart-rending cry, she fell to the floor, pale and motionless.

"Is she dead! Mon Dieu! Ma chere fille, speak to me." And then raising her death-pale head a little, he poured some of the spirits into her mouth. This restored her, but there was an almost vacant look in her eye for many minutes, which wrung his heart. "Sit up my pet and we will talk together. I will no longer play the inhuman monster by disguises and deceit."

"Then you will be frank?" she said, her eyes brightening.

"I swear it. Now this man has conceived a violent passion for you, and I am to press his suit, to alienate your affections from Monsieur Scott, if you entertain such feelings, and to win you over to Monsieur Riel. He is to visit us within a brief period, and when he comes he will expect me to be able to report marked progress. He will make a second visit, and he has sworn that triumph alone will satisfy him then. If things fall not out in this wise, I am promised his vengeance. He declares that our intimacy with young Scott, and the visit paid us by the homme mauvais Mair, who is an unscrupulous agent of the Canadian Government, would justify extreme measures against us; and if I mistake not the man, his intention is to arm hundreds of our people, proclaim a martial law, and establish himself as head and judge. I am certain that he would not hesitate to take the most lawless steps. Indeed,

I should not regard as safe either my own life or your honour. Such then being the facts, what are we to do?"

"God is good; let us first of all put our trust in Him. Then let us examine the means which He has given us to meet the evil. Now, my plan is that I shall in the first instance affect to yield with grief to such proposals as you at first make to me. Let there be a surrender of Monsieur Scott—" Here she blushed so deeply that all her sweet-rounded cheek, and her neck, and her delicious little shell-like ears, became a crimson, deep as her bodice— "and a consent to entertain as favourably as I can the suit of M. Riel. Meanwhile we can see what is the next best step. I do not think that we have much to dread by leaving Red River. We can go to your brother who lives across the border, and I am certain that he will be delighted to harbour us till the tempest blows over. I believe that this rising will rage for a brief season only, when it must yield to the arm of the Canadian authorities. M. Riel is a fanatic, and counts not the perilousness of his undertaking. He will succeed at the first, I doubt not. You will hear of slaughtered whites, and others who have incurred his private vengeance. He will lord it over all like a tyrant, till he sees the bayonets from Canada, when he will take good care to get out of the way." Her father saw that her views were sound, and consented to take her advice; but who was to acquaint his brother with their needs, and to learn if he could afford a harbourage?

"Paul can go. He can take the pony and ride the distance in twelve hours." So it was agreed, and Marie busied herself with the linen of her brother, and sewed missing buttons upon his clothes. In the evening, when all were seated at supper, a young half-breed who had long been an intimate friend at the house of Marie's father, and who cast many a languishing eye upon the piquant Violette, came in. There was much concern in his face, and it was some time before he knew how to begin to break the news which he possessed.

"Monsieur Riel was at my father's house to-day, and he talked long there. He is not your friend," looking at Jean. "He declares that you are in league with the enemies of our colony, and has asked my father to keep a strict watch on the doings of every member of your family. I know that he talked in the same strain at every house he visited; and I think there is no threshold in our settlement that he hasn't crossed. About twenty-five young men have declared their willingness to follow him in any exploit. They met upon a field this afternoon and drilled for a couple of hours. One of them told me,"—the speaker now turned his gaze half toward Marie—"not an hour ago that their first business would be to settle affairs with Messieurs Mair and Scott, whom they declare are enemies of Red River, and spies of the Canadian government. I should not wonder if these two men were secured to-night; and if this be so, and I am any judge of human malevolence, Riel will have them shot." The colour had gone out of Marie's cheek, and there was a terrified gleam in her eye.

"Can nothing be done," she asked, "to apprise them of the miscreant's designs?"

"I regret that I can do nothing; you know how gladly I would were it in my power. Every man between twenty-one and sixty years in our settlement, has been called out to attend a meeting to be held during the evening in the school-house, to discuss the situation. One Lepine, a bosom friend of Monsieur Riel, is to tell us what we are to do. I, therefore, will have to be present."

"I shall go," said young Paul. "I can reach Willow grove long before the moon is up, and give warning to Monsieur Scott. But Monsieur Mair has to take care of himself. I would very gladly assist in his capture, or for that matter be well pleased to be one of a firing party to dispatch his insolent, insulting life." The young lad's cheeks were burning with indignation. "I think Monsieur Riel is an impostor, although the cause which he has espoused is a holy one. But this Mair, after receiving our hospitalities turns and holds us up to the ridicule, contempt and pity of the world. Under obligation must we ever remain to Monsieur Scott, but beyond this, he is a true gentleman, and incapable of the remotest sympathy with the mean unmanliness of this Monsieur Mair."

Paul, was a tall, handsome lad, with large, spirited, brown eyes. He was in his eighteenth year, but had the manly address of twenty-one. His sister's gratitude gleamed in her eyes. When he was ready to go out to saddle his pony, she put her arms about him and kissed him.

"Que Dieu benisse, mon bon frere. Bon voyage!" and she watched him, I doubt not praying, though her ruby lips moved not, for him, and for her lover, till the flitting figure of himself and his fleet-limbed pony was lost in the dusk that had already gathered over the plain… That evening when Paul returned he came not alone. Another steed and rider were there, and beyond, in the shadow of a grove of cottonwood stood a party of a dozen horsemen. Marie heard the double tramp, and with some terror drew to the window to see who was approaching. But her apprehensions suddenly vanished, and a flush came over her face.

CHAPTER VII.

"Mon pere, it is Paul, and there is with him Monsieur Scott; why, I wonder, has he come?" While the question yet remained unanswered, Paul entered the room accompanied by young Scott.

"Monsieur will explain the cause of his visit," Paul said.

"Monsieur and mademoiselle," young Scott began, inclining his head first to the father and then to the daughter, "as you may expect, only great urgency brought me here under these circumstances. A half-breed to whom I did a kindness since coming to the territories, is one of Monsieur Riel's agents, and is in the confidence of that dangerous person. He tells me that this very night, probably before the rise of the moon, a party is to surround your house, and make you and your daughter captives. The charge against you is, that you are both in league with Canadian spies, and enemies of Red River. One of the said spies is myself! It appears that you are to be taken to the common jail; and mademoiselle Marie is to be lodged in the house of a Metis hag, who is a depraved instrument of Riel's will. Therefore, I have brought hither an escort sufficient to accomplish your safe retreat to some refuge beyond the American frontier. Paul tells me that you had proposed going to your brother's. I do not consider this a safe plan. Your malignant persecutor will very speedily learn from your neighbours all information respecting the existence of relatives, and where they reside. You would be no safer from the vengeance of this monster in adjacent, thinly settled American territory, than you would be in Red River. Will you therefore come with me to my uncle's in a town not far beyond the line?—only too happy will he be to serve you in your need." The proposal was very gladly accepted. Tears stood in old Jean's eyes; and I doubt not that they came there when he began to reflect that, but for Marie, he should now have been acting in league with his miscreant persecutor against this noble, generous-hearted young fellow.

Within an hour, most of the little valuables in the dear old homestead, which neither Jean nor Marie ever again expected to see, were made up into small packs, each one to be carried by one of the escorts. With a deep sigh Marie looked at the home of her happy youth, drowsing in the deep shadow of the oaks, and then mounted her horse. All that night she rode by her lover's side, and stole many a glance of admiring pride at his handsome, manly figure. When they were a couple of hours out, a dusky yellow appeared in the south-east, and then the bright, greenish-yellow rim of the Autumn moon appeared, and began to flood the illimitable prairie with a thick, wizard light.

"So this miscreant has been hunting you, Marie?" said the young man, for both had unconsciously dropped in rear. "I did not like his glances this morning, and had resolved to keep my eyes upon him. I suppose, ma petite, if I had the right to keep you from the fans of water-mills, that I also hold the right of endeavouring to preserve you from a man whose arms would be worse than the rending wheel?" She said nothing, but there was gratitude enough in her eye to reward for the most daring risk that man ever run.

"You do not love this sooty persecutor, do you, ma chere?"—and then, seeing that such a question pained and confused her, he said, "Hush now, ma petite fille; I shall not tease you any more." The confusion passed away, and her little olive face brightened, as does the moon when the cloud drifts off its disc.

"I am very glad. O, if you only knew how I shudder at the sound of his name!"

"There now, let us forget about him, I can protect you from him; can I not?" and he reined his horse closer to hers, and leaned tenderly over towards the girl. She said nothing, for she was very much confused. But the confusion was less embarrassment than a bewildered feeling of delight. But for the dull thud, thud of the hoofs upon the sod, her escort might plainly enough have heard the riotous beating of the little maiden's heart.

"And now, about that flower which I gave you this morning. What did you do with it?"

"Ah, Monsieur, where were your eyes? I have worn it in my hair all day. It is there now; it was there when you came to our cottage this evening."

"Ah, I see. I am concerned with your head,—not with your heart. Is that it, ma petite bright eye? You know our white girls wear the flowers we give them under their throats, or upon their bosom. This they do as a sign that the donor occupies a place in their heart." He did not perceive in the dusky moonlight, that he was covering her with confusion. Upon no point was this little maiden so sensitive, as when it was revealed to her that a particular habit or act of hers differed from that of the civilized white girl. Her dear little heart was almost bursting with shame, and this thought was running through her mind.

"Oh! what a savage I must seem in his eyes." Her own unspoken words seemed to burn through her whole body. "But how could I know where to wear my rose? I have read in English books that gentle ladies wear them there." And these lines of Tennyson came running through her head.

"She went by dale, and she went by down,
  With a single rose in her hair."

And they gave her some relief, for she thought, after all, that he might be only joking When the blood had gone back from her forehead, she turned towards her lover, who had been looking at her since speaking with somewhat of a tender expression in his mischievous eyes.

"Do white girls never wear roses in their hair? I thought they did. Can it be wrong for me to wear mine in the same place?"

"Ah, my little barbarian, you do not understand me. If an old bachelor, whose head shone like the moon there in the sky, were to give to some blithe young belle a rose or a lily, she would, most likely, twist it in her hair; but if some other hand had presented the flower, one whose eye was brighter, whose step was quicker, whose laugh was cheerier, whose years were fewer; in short, ma chere Marie, if some one for whom she cared just a little bit more than for any other man that walked over the face of creation, had presented it to her, she would not put it in her hair. No, my little unsophisticated one, she would feel about with her unerring fingers, for the spot nearest her heart, and there she would fasten the gift. Now, ma Marie, suppose you had possessed all this information this morning when I gave you the flower, where would you have pinned it?"

"Nobody has ever done so much for me as has Monsieur. He leaped into the flood, risking his life to save mine. I would be an ungrateful girl, then, if I did not think more of him than of any other man; therefore, I would have pinned your flower on the spot nearest my heart," Then, deftly, and before he could determine what her supple arms and nimble little brown fingers were about, she had disengaged the lily from her hair, and pinned it upon her bosom. "There now, Monsieur, is it in the right place?" and she looked at him with a glance exhibiting the most curious commingling of innocence and coquetry.

"I cannot answer. I do not think that you understand me yet. If the act of saving you from drowning were to determine the place you should wear the rose, then the head, as you first chose, was the proper spot, Do you know what the word love means?"

"O, I could guess, perhaps, if I don't know. I have heard a good deal about it, and Violette, who is desperately fond of a handsome young Frenchman, has explained it so fully to me, that I think I know. Yes, Monsieur, I *do* know."

"Well, you little rogue, it takes one a long time to find out whether you do or not. In fact I am not yet quite satisfied on the point. However, let me suppose that you do know what love is; the all-consuming sort, the kind that sighs like the very furnace. Well, that part of the statement is clear. Then, supposing that a flower is worn over the heart only to express love, of the sort I mentioned, for the donor, where would you, with full knowledge of this fact, have pinned the flower that I plucked for you this morning?"

"Since I do not understand the meaning of the word love with very great clearness,—I think Monsieur has expressed the doubt that I do understand it—I would not have known where to pin the flower. I would not have worn it at all. I would, Monsieur, have set it in a goblet, and taking my stitching, would have gazed upon it all the day, and prayed my guardian angel to give me some hint as to where I ought to put it on."

"You little savage, you have eluded me again. Do you remember me telling you that some day, if you found out for me a couple of good flocks of turkeys, I would bring you some coppers?"

"I do."

"Well, if you discovered a hundred flocks now, I would not give you one." And then he leaned towards her again as if his lips yearned for hers; but his love of mischief was too strong for every other desire. For her part, she took him exactly as she should have done. She never pouted;—If she had done so, I fancy that there would have been soon an end of the wild, boyish, sunny raillery.

"Hallo! Little one, we are away, away in the rear. Set your pony going, for we must keep up with our escort." Away they went over the level plain, through flowers of every name and dye, the fresh, exquisite, autumn breeze bearing the scent of the myriad petals upon their faces. After a sharp gallop over about three miles of plain, they overtook the main body of the escort.

They now reached the border, and the pavements of the little town of Pembina rang with the hoofs of their horses. Away still to the south, they rode through the glorious autumn night, under the calm, bountiful moon.

"Now, Monsieur Riel, I think we are some distance from your foul talons," Scott said, as turning in his saddle, he saw the steeples of Pembina, gloom-wrapped, almost sunk in the horizon. "I fancy I can hear the curses of his willing tools in the air, after they swooped down upon your cottage, Marie, and found the inmates flown."

"What is your uncle's cottage like, Monsieur Scott?"

"It is not unlike your own. It is in a grove of pines, and a happy brook goes chattering by it all the summer. Will you come fishing in it with me, ma petite?"

"Oui, avec le plus grand plaisir, Monsieur," and she looked so happy, there was so much sun in her eyes, so many divine little dimples in her cheek, in contemplation of all the promised happiness, that it would not require much keenness to discover the secret of the dear little maiden.

"Of course, you shall fish with a pin-hook. I am not going to see you catch yourself with one of the barbed hooks, like those which I shall use."

"O, Monsieur Scott! Why will you always treat me as a baby!" and there was the most delicate, yet an utterly indescribable sort of reproach in her voice and attitude, as she spoke these words.

"Then it is not a baby by any means," and he looked with undisguised admiration upon the maiden, with all the mystic grace and perfect development of her young womanhood. "It is a woman, a perfect little woman, a fairer a sweeter, my own mignonette, than any girl ever seen in this part of the plains since first appeared here human footprint."

"O, Monsieur is now gone to the other extreme. He is talking dangerously; for he will make me vain."

"Does the ceaseless wooing of the sweet wild rose by soft winds, make that blossom vain? or is the moon spoilt because all the summer night ten thousand streams running under it sing to it unnumbered praises? As easy, ma Marie, to make vain the rose or the moon as to turn your head by telling your perfections."

"Monsieur covers me with confusion!" and the little sweet told the truth. But it was a confusion very exquisite to her. It sang like entrancing music through her veins; and gave her a delightful delirium about the temples, flow fair all the glorious great round of the night, and the broad earth lit by the moon, seemed to her now, with the music of his words coursing through her being. Everything was transfigured by a holy beauty, for Love had sanctified it, and clothed it with his own mystic, wonderful garments. It was with poor Marie, then, as it has some time or other been with us all: when every bird that sang, every leaf that whispered, had in its tone a cadence caught from the one loved voice. I have seen the steeple strain, and rock, and heard the bells peal out in all their clangourous melody, and I have fancied that this delirious ecstasy of sound that bathed the earth and went up to heaven was the voice of one slim girl with dimples and sea-green eyes.

The mischievous young Scotchman had grown more serious than Marie had ever seen him before.

"I hope, my child, that you will be happy here; the customs of the people differ from yours, but your nature is receptive to everything good and elevated, so that I am certain you will soon grow to cherish our civilization."

I must say here for the benefit of the drivelling, cantankerous critic, with a squint in his eye, who never looks for anything good in a piece of writing, but is always on the search for a flaw, that I send passages from Tennyson floating through my Marie's brain with good justification. She had received a very fair education at a convent in Red River. She could speak and write both French and English with tolerable accuracy; and she could with her supple, tawny little fingers, produce a nice sketch of a prairie tree-clump, upon a sheet of cartridge paper, or a piece of birch rind.

Young Scott was all the while growing more serious, and even becoming pathetic, which is a sign of something very delicious, and not uncommon, when you are travelling under a bewitching moon, in company with a more bewitching maiden.

"I wish I could be with you during the early part of your stay here, for I could do much toward reconciling you to your new life."

"And are you not going to stay with us?" Her voice sounded somewhat like a restrained cry of pain.

"No Marie, my child, I have to return to the territories."

"But that wicked man will work his vengeance upon you."

"It is just to meet that wicked man upon his own ground that I go back. It is to thwart him, to cast in my strength on the side of peace, in the interest of those fertile plains, that I return. You do not suppose that this licentious fanatic can ultimately prevail against the will of the people of Canada, against the military force of the Empire of Great Britain. The sovereign of our mighty realm tolerates in no land any dispute of her authority, and this mad uprising will be crushed as I might stamp put the feeble splutter of a bed-room taper. There are without the intervention of outside force at all, enough of brave and loyal whitemen to overthrow this scurvy miscreant; and my immediate task is to do the little that lies in my power to incite them to their duty. When my work is done, when the plains are cleared of the mutinous, blind, unreasoning hordes whom this cunning, vainglorious upstart has called away from their peaceful homesteads, I will return, my darling little girl, with the tidings; and I shall bring you back to the spot where you grew up pure and artless as the lily that brightens the pond upon which we have so often paddled our birch together. What the days after that may have in store for us I know not."

"Ah, I shall be very dreary in your absence, Monsieur Scott."

"And I, my dear girl, shall be not less dreary without you. I believe you have regarded yourself as a mere plaything in my eyes. Why, ma chere, all of my heart you have wholly and irrevocably. One of your dear hands is more precious, more sacred to me, than any other girl whom mine eyes have ever seen. Do you remember the definition of love that I tried to give you? Well, I gave it from my own experience. With such a love, my prairie flower, do I love you. It is fit now, that we are so soon to part, that I should tell you this: and you will, know that every blow I strike, every noble deed I do shall be for the approbation of the dear heart distant from me in American territory. I have said that the hours of absence will be dreary; but there will be beyond the the darkest of them one hope which shall blaze like a star through the night, and that is that I shall soon be able to call my Marie my sweet, sweet bride. Now, my beloved, if that wished for time had come, and I were to say, 'Will you be mine, Marie,' what would you answer?"

"I did not think that it would be necessary for Monsieur to ask me that question," she answered shyly, her beautiful eyes cast down; "I thought he knew."

"My own little hunted pet!" He checked his horse, and seized the bridle of Marie's pony, till the two animals stood close together. Then he kissed the girl upon her sweet virgin lips, murmuring low,

"My love."

The next morning he was away, and Marie sat sad by the strange brook that ho had told her about. Old Jean was very contented, but now that he had nought to do, ha babbled all day about the wars; and thanked the Virgin that himself and his child had escaped the clutches of the Rebel leader. Paul speedily obtained employment harvesting on a large farm near by, and after a little old Jean began to be extremely useful to his kind host. But tying sheaves was not the occupation, at this tumultuous time, that young Paul's heart would have chosen. For how he longed to be in the fray! to stand, side by side, with his young comrade, Luc, fighting for the honour and independence of Riviere Rouge. It was only, after the most tedious argument, that he could be prevailed upon to stay; and it was Thomas Scott, who had so overcome him.

"You know the designs that this monster harbours," that young man had said to Paul. "You are foolish enough to count now on his patriotism, and to imagine that he would welcome you to his ranks. He would act far differently: he would probably spare you, provided that you lent yourself to his evil designs. If you refused to do this, he would very probably shoot you as a traitor to your country."

As for Riel, it may seem that his conduct in deciding in one hour, to use Marie's father as a tool, and, during the next, projecting a plan which defeated the very end which he had in view, was absolutely illogical, and unreasonable; and that it is the narrator whose skill is at fault. But I have been at pains to give this occurrence at length, for the very purpose of revealing the unstaid, unreasoning character of Riel, and how far passion and impulse will carry him away from sound understanding.

As for the Arch-agitator, the spirits taken at the house of old Jean, had raised the savage part of his blood to the highest pitch of unreasoning and confident passion. All obstacles seemed to disappear, and he saw with the same glance the gratification of his passion and of his revenge.

"Take the horses," he had said to his confidant, "before the moon rises. Approach the house softly, and carefully surround it. The girl must be treated with respect. You know where to leave her."

"Oui, Monsieur," and the slavish fanatic went to do the vile bidding.

For some hours M. Riel went among the Metis, perfecting his plans, but towards midnight he ordered his horse, and, with a lurid light in his eye, set off for the hut of the half-breed hag where he expected his ruffianly emissaries would have placed Marie before his arrival. But the cabin was desolate, save for the figure of an ill-featured old woman, who, when she heard hoof-beats approach, came to the door peering out into the night.

"Has the expected yet arrived?" he asked, a half-puzzled expression in his face.

"No, Monsieur."

"Curses! What can have happened? They should have been here two hours ago. It is now three o'clock." Then he alighted and strode about for half an hour over the dim-lit sward, thrusting out his head every few seconds, in the direction from which the party should come. But still no sound, no sight, of any horseman. He now began to storm and blaspheme, and would remind anybody who saw him of some wild beast foiled of his prey. Presently, he observed a long distance off upon the plain, a figure which he believed was moving. Was this only a poplar or a cotton-wood tree? He got upon his knees, and put his ear to the ground; the soft thud of a horse's hoof vibrated under his ear, and he was satisfied.

"But there is only one horseman. What can it mean?" He could not bear the suspense, and flinging himself upon his horse, he galloped out to meet the advancing stranger. It was soon told. The inmates had escaped, evidently long before the party got to the dwelling. The embers were very low on the hearth. Every article of value had been removed, and there were the prints of many hoofs near the cottage.

"Scott has foiled me!" and the outwitted tyrant-libertine swore the most terrible oaths, that he would be revenged.

"Off," he said to his confidant. "You must scour Red River over to find these fugitives. Wherever you see the girl, seize her, and bring her hither. The people must all know that she is a spy, and leagued with our most deadly enemies to thwart our cause. As for the father, catch him too, though I should not fret, if, in the capture, a stray bullet or two went singing through his head. Above all, Scott must be captured," and this was to himself, "let me lay hands upon him!"

The horseman was riding off.

"Stop! This old Jean has relatives in the territory; and with one of these he may be taking refuge."

"I do not think that this is likely, Monsieur. But I learnt, and it was the prosecution of these enquiries among Jean's nearest neighbours, that kept me late in reaching you, that he has a brother in Pembina. Now in that direction did the hoof-marks of the party lead."

"I see. He has gone there, counting on safety beyond the lines; but he leans upon a hollow reed. Let me see: to-morrow at the convention, next day at the grand parade of arms. Yes, on Tuesday evening, take with you forty men to Pembina. Of course, you go there with all speed, and locate the residence. Then on Tuesday night, when you enter the city, surround the house by a sortie You will have nothing to fear from the citizens, they have no force there to oppose yours, and if they had you could accomplish your mission so suddenly that you might be on the prairie with your prize before they had their arms in their hands." The horseman rode off, and the Rebel was alone.

We have seen that Mr. McDougall had appointed his Deputy Colonel Dennis, as Conservator of the peace, and authorized him to organize a force, and put down the Rebellion. The English and Scotch settlers, almost to a man, sympathized with the interdicted governor; yet they did not care to bring themselves into conflict with men, with whom, for years past, they had lived in the most friendly relationship, unless some great necessity arose. As for Riel, they regarded him as an ambitious, short-sighted demagogue, who palmed off his low cunning for brilliant leadership, upon the credulous half-breeds. Nevertheless, a large number of these settlers declared their readiness to march under Colonel Dennis, and disperse the nest of rebels at Fort Garry. I need hardly say that most of the Irish settlers were heart and soul with Riel. It was not that they had any particular grievance to resent, or any grievance at all for that matter. It was as natural to them to rise in revolt, since the rising meant resistance to the lawful authority, as it is for the little duck first cast into the pond, to swim. A red haired, pug-nosed Irishman, coming to New York, leaped ashore and asked,

"Is there a guvernment in this counthry?"

"There is."

"Thin I'm opposed to it."

Much the same was it in the North-West, and the violent, blustering ruffian O'Donoghue was the mouthpiece, the leader, the type of that class of the people.

A number of loyal Scotch and English, therefore, did arise, and they were known as the Portage party. This was some months after the night that we last saw Riel thwarted upon the prairies. In that connection it only remains to be said that the mission of the confidant to Pembina was fruitless; and the Rebel gnashed his teeth that his desires and his revenge had all been baulked. He had heard, however, that Thomas Scott was abroad through his territories; and that he had enlisted under the banner of Colonel Dennis,—which was the truth. What galled him most was, that in case he should succeed in getting Scott into his hands, he had no proofs that would be regarded as sufficient evidence upon which to proceed with the extreme of vengeance toward him. Yet his orders stood unchanged:

"Wherever you find Thomas Scott seize him; and convey him to Fort Garry." On the sixth of December the confidant came into the tyrant's presence and said:

"We have caught Scott." [Footnote: I take the following from Begg's "History of the North-West Rebellion," p. 161: "About this time (6th December), the French arrested and imprisoned Mr. Thomas Scott, Mr. A. McArthur, and Mr. Wm. Hallet. Mr. Scott, it appears, had been one of the party assembled in Schultz's house, but had afterwards left; and no other reason for his arrest is known, except his having enrolled under Colonel Dennis. Mr. McArthur, was, it is said, confined on suspicion of acting secretly on behalf of Mr. McDougall; and Mr. Hallet, for his activity in assisting and advising Colonel Dennis."] The Rebel leader's eye gleamed with a wolfish light.

"Is he in the Fort?"

"Yes."

"Bon! I shall be there presently." So without any delay he proceeded to the Fort, and entered the apartment where young Scott was confined.

"Ah, Monsieur! This is where you are?"

"Yes, you tyrannical ruffian. But I shall not be here for long." Riel curbed the mad blood which had leaped to his temples.

"Monsieur shall not be here long, if he chooses to accept conditions upon which he may be free."

"Come, for curiosity sake, let us hear the proposals; I am certain that they are foul. Yet, as I say, I am anxious to hear them."

"Monsieur must be reasonable. There is no good purpose to be served by railing at me."

"That is true. You are too infamous a miscreant to be shamed or made better by reproaches."

"Nevertheless, I shall proceed to business, Monsieur. Do you know where old Jean and his daughter have taken up their abode?"

"I do."

"So I suspected. If you will let me know their place of abode, that I may give them my guarantee for their personal safety if they return to their home—as I understand that through some unfounded fear of me they fled, and I am anxious to stand well in the affections of all my people—I shall permit you forthwith to leave this Fort."

"Contemptible villain, liar and tyrant, I will *not* reveal to you. Begone. By heaven! if you stand there I shall bury my hands in your foul, craven throat."

"Take care, Monsieur," was all M. Riel said, as he left Scott's presence. But his eye burned like a fiend's. The agitator, with a spirit of the most devilish rage consuming him, nevertheless went on to forward the general movement. His first great step was against the followers of Colonel Dennis, who had banded together and posted themselves in the house of Dr. Schultz, a very prominent settler. They had gathered here with arms in their hands, but they seemed like a lot of little children, without any purpose. There was no moral cohesion among them, and there was no force either to lead or to drive them. They were not long thus ridiculously impounded, when they began to look at one another, as if to ask:

"*Quis furores o cives?*"

They were not alone unprepared and undetermined to go up to Fort Garry, and fight the greasy Rebel and his followers, but they were by no means certain as to what they should do were the enemy to come against them. And this is just the very thing that the enterprising Monsieur Riel proposed to do. It is said that about this time he was often found reading books describing the sudden and unexpected military movements of Napoleon. And I have not the remotest doubt that the diseased vanity of the presumptuous crank enabled him to see a likeness in himself to the Scourge of Nations. So he said to his men:

"We shall go down and capture this Dennis' geese-pound. Better turn out in good force, with your arms, though I am quite certain that you can capture the whole caboose with broom-sticks." So the Metis thronged after his heels, and surrounded the Schultz mansion with its "congregation of war spirits." Of course there is something to be said for the gathering together of these loyal people here, as there is for the issuing of the proclamation by the citizens of London, per the mouth of the three tailors. Beyond was Fort Garry, unlawfully seized by Riel, and now unlawfully invested by his troops. This was, therefore, a menace to the unlawful combination at the fort. At once the agitator began to dictate terms. If they would come out of their ridiculous hive, and surrender their arms, he would suffer no harm whatever to befall them; but content himself with merely taking them all in a lump, and locking them up prisoners in the fort. He would, however, insist upon other formalities; and, therefore, exhibited a declaration which he would ask them to sign. By this document each man would bind himself to rise no more, but to submit to the authority of the Provisional Government. There was very little parleying. Each brave loyalist took the paper, and put his name to it. [Footnote *] Dr. O'Donnell was the first to sign his name, and after he had done the rest followed and with much credit to the celerity of their penmanship. Then they all moved out and were escorted up to Fort Garry, where they were held for a considerable period, despite the prayers of prominent persons who had taken no active part on either side, for their liberation.

[* Footnote: I take the following from Mr. Begg's History of the Rebellion: "In the meantime, there were from two to three hundred armed French half-breeds, as well as a number of lookers-on, around and outside the building; and it is said that a couple of mounted cannon (six pounders) were drawn outside the walls of Fort Garry, ready to be used in case of an assault upon the besieged premises.

"When all those in the house had signed, and the surrender handed to Riel, he said that there were two signatures not on the list, which ought to be there—and which he insisted upon having. These were the names of James Mulligan and Charles Garrett. A guard from the French party was therefore sent to hunt up those two men; and in a short time they returned with the individuals they had been in search of. As soon as this had been done, the prisoners were taken out and marched to Fort Garry; and the following ladies, who, during the siege, had nobly resolved upon remaining by the side of their husbands, also insisted upon accompanying them to Fort Garry.

"The following are the names of the ladies: Mrs. Schultz, Mrs. Mair, Mrs. O'Donnell; and as the first named lady was ill, probably from the excitement of the past few days, a sleigh was procured, and Dr. Schultz himself drew her along in it, behind the rest of the prisoners. When they reached Fort Garry, Mr. J. H. McTavish, accountant in the Hudson Bay Company service, kindly offered to give up his private quarters for the use of the married men and their families, and thus made things more comfortable for the ladies."]

CHAPTER VIII.

In the meantime, the Government at Ottawa had convinced itself that affairs were in a pretty bad mess in the North-West. Therefore they dispatched, with olive branches, two commissioners to treat with the malcontents. It is hardly worth while to mention the names of these two gentlemen, though I may as well do so. They were Vicar-General Thibeault, this prelate, I understand, being a relative of the gentleman who produced the life of Sir Charles Tupper, and Colonel DeSalaberry. Mr. Donald A. Smith, the chief officer of the Hudson Bay Company, was also dispatched. He was instructed to inquire into and report upon the cause of the disturbances and also to assist Governor McTavish, or to relieve him, altogether of duties should ill health have incapacitated him. Mr. Smith arrived in due season at the settlement, and sought an interview with the Rebel leader in Fort Garry. M. Riel very readily admitted him; and then turned the keys upon him. It was a very great pity that it was not upon some members of the beautiful government at Ottawa that he had the opportunity of fastening the locks! There were now about sixty prisoners in the fort; the British ensign had been hauled down, and the flag of the Provisional Government, a combination of fleurs de-lys and shamrocks, hoisted in its stead. When the news got abroad that an agent had come from Canada to treat with the people on behalf of the Canadian Government, that Mr. McDougall was in disfavour with the Dominion ministry, and had returned to Ottawa, M. Riel's influence began to diminish sensibly.

"Let us hear what Donald Smith has to say to us," they began to cry; and the Arch Rebel was fain to consent. A monster meeting of 1,100 people was held in the open air, with the thermometer twenty degrees below zero. Riel and his followers were not satisfied with the terms of the Dominion agent; and the arch disturber had made up his mind not to be satisfied. Yet he was not secure in his position, for there was much writhing among hosts of his followers under his tyrannical caprices. Sometimes he broke loose from all civilized restraint, and acted like a mad savage. Governor McTavish, who was reaching the last stages of consumption, for some reason incurred the ill-will of the autocrat. One might have supposed that a man tottering on the grave's brink would have been secure from violence and insult; but the heartless Rebel ruffian was insensible to every human impulse. Bursting into the chamber of the sick man, he raged like a wild bull, stamped upon the floor, and declared that he would have him shot before midnight. Then telling off a guard he sent them to invest the house.

His rage cooled down after a little, and the murderous threat was not carried into execution. I have said that the loyalty and obedience of his entire followers were, so far, by no means assured. Hundreds who sympathized with the uprising, and in the beginning expressed admiration for his courage and daring, began to be shocked at his tyranny, and to hold aloof. This was the reason, we may be sure, that some of the revengeful threats which he, about this time made, were not carried into effect. He held long counsel with his military leader, Lepine.

"How does the sentiment of the settlement go now? Do they disapprove of my severe measures?"

"They do, Monsieur; and I am inclined to think that you will be obliged to show some generosity, even toward your worst enemies, to maintain the confidence and sympathy of your followers."

"Suppose I release these prisoners?"

"I know of nothing more popular that you could do."

"But Scott? He is my deadliest enemy. It is to give a colour of justification to my attitude towards him that I have incarcerated the rest."

"Even him, Monsieur, I think it would be advisable now to let him depart with the rest. I am quite certain that he will before long, moved by his hatred of yourself, commit some act that will justify you in according to him very stern sort of punishment.

"Be it so. I shall let them all go. But remember: you never must allow this man to pass from under your eye."

Meanwhile poor Marie was far away, sighing all the day for some word from her lover. She had heard that they had captured him and locked him in a dungeon. A terrible fever seized her, and she cried out in her delirium to take her to her lover. For many days after the fire of her illness had cooled, she lay between life and death like some fitful shadow; but when a letter came to her, in the dear writing that she so well knew, announcing that he was once more free, the enfeebled blood began to stir in her veins, and a faint tint of rose began to appear on the wasted cheek.

"I will run over and see my little love during the first breathing time that offers," he wrote. "I hope, ma amie, you are not sorrowing at my absence. No hour passes over me, whether wake or dreaming, that I do not sigh for my darling Marie; but I am consoled with the thought that when the turmoil is ended, when this land of tumult and tyranny has become a region of peace and fruitful industry, I will be able to bring my darling back to her dear old home; and in a little wed her there, and then take her to my arms for ever."

This was very sweet tidings to the desolate girl. She read the letter over and over till she could repeat every word of the eight large pages which it contained. When she began to grow stronger she would keep it in her lap all day, and touch it tenderly as a young mother would her sleeping babe. Before blowing out her lamp in the night she would kiss the letter, and put it under her pillow. When she opened her large bright eyes in the morning she would take it, kiss it, and read it once again.

During all this time the fire of Riel's two-fold passion was not burning lower:—nay, it was growing stronger. His aim now was to make himself such a ruler and master in the settlement that every word of his should be as law, and that no man, not all the people, might disobey his command or censure his action.

"So Thomas Scott is to marry her, when the strife ends," he would speculate. "Ah, Monsieur Scott, if to that time you defer your nuptials, they shall take place in heaven —or in hell." For the furtherance of his diabolical personal aims he now began to assume a benignant, fatherly tone, and when he issued his famous "Proclamation to the people of the North-West," everybody was struck by the calmness, the restraint, and even the dignity of its language. [Footnote *1] He likewise endeavoured to show that he was not a disturber whose only mission was to pull down. Through his instrumentality, and at his suggestion in every one of its details, a Bill of Rights, [Footnote *2] was drawn up, and published to the people. This document set forth little more than what would be regarded as legitimate requests.

[*1 Footnote: This document was as follows:—"Let the assembly of twenty-eight representatives, which met on the 9th March, be dear to the people of Red River! That assembly has shown itself worthy of great confidence. It has worked in union. The members devoted themselves to the public interests, and yielded only to sentiments of good will, duty and generosity. Thanks to that noble conduct, public authority is now strong. That strength will be employed to sustain and protect the people of the country.

"To-day the Government pardons all those whom political differences led astray only for a time. Amnesty will be generously accorded to all those who will submit to the Government; who will discountenance or inform against dangerous gatherings.

"From this day forth the public highways are open.

"The Hudson Bay Company can now resume business. Themselves contributing to the public good, they circulate their money as of old. They pledge themselves to that course.

"The attention of the Government is also directed very specially to the northern part of the country, in order that trade there may not receive any serious check, and peace in the Indian districts may thereby he all the more securely maintained.

"The disastrous war which at one time threatened us, has left among us fears and various deplorable results. But let the people feel reassured.

"Elevated by the Grace of Providence and the suffrages of my fellow-citizens to the highest position in the Government of my country, I proclaim that peace reigns in our midst this day. The Government will take every precaution to prevent this peace from being disturbed.

"While internally all is thus returning to order, externally, also, matters are looking favourable. Canada invites the Red River people to an amicable arrangement. She offers to guarantee us our rights, and to give us a place in the Confederation equal to that of any other Province.

"Identified with the Provisional Government, our national will, based upon justice, shall be respected.

"Happy country, to have escaped many misfortunes that were prepared for her! In seeing her children on the point of a war, she recollects the old friendship which used to bind them, and by the ties of the same patriotism she has re-united them again for the sake of preserving their lives, their liberties, and their happiness.

"Let us remain united and we shall be happy. With strength of unity we shall retain prosperity.

"O, my fellow-countrymen, without distinction of language, or without distinction of creed—keep my words in your hearts! If ever the time should unhappily come when another division should take place amongst us, such as foreigners heretofore sought to create, that will be the signal for all the disasters which we have had the happiness to avoid.

"In order to prevent similar calamities, the Government will treat with all the severity of the law those who will dare again to compromise the public security. It is ready to act against the disorder of parties as well as against that of individuals. But let us hope rather that extreme measures will be unknown and that the lessons of the past will guide us in the future.

"LOUIS RIEL.

"Government House,

"Fort Garry, April 9th, 1870."]

[*2 Footnote: This document claimed:—

"1st. The right to elect our own Legislature.

"2. The Legislature to have power to pass all laws, local to the Territory, over the veto of the Executive, by a two-thirds vote.

"3. No Act of the Dominion Parliament (local to this Territory) to be binding on the people until sanctioned by their representatives.

"4. All sheriffs, magistrates, constables, &c., &c., to be elected by the people—a free homestead pre-emption law.

"5. A portion of the public lands to be appropriated to the benefit of schools, the building of roads, bridges, and parish buildings.

"6. A guarantee to connect Winnipeg by rail with the nearest line of railroad—the land grant for such road or roads to be subject to the Legislature of the Territory.

"7. For four years the public expenses of the Territory, civil, military and municipal, to be paid out of the Dominion Treasury.

"8. The military to be composed of the people now existing in the Territory.

"9. The French and English language to be common in the Legislature and Council, and all public documents and Acts of Legislature to be published in both languages.

"10. That the Judge of the Superior Court speak French and English.

"11. Treaties to be concluded and ratified between the Government and several tribes of Indians of this Territory, calculated to I insure peace in the future.

"12. That all privileges, customs and usages existing at the time of the transfer, be respected.

"13. That these rights be guaranteed by Mr. McDougall before he be admitted into this Territory.

"14. If he have not the power himself to grant them, he must get an Act of Parliament passed expressly securing us these rights: and, until such Act be obtained, he must stay outside the Territory."]

His followers soon began to forget his late manifestation of tyranny and violence, and his enemies found themselves silenced by his restraint, and the wisdom of his declarations. Yet the rebel leader for many reasons, one of which is very well known to the reader, was one of the unhappiest of men. Besides the matter at his heart he lived hourly in mortal dread of bodily harm. In the dead of night he would waken, start suddenly from his bed and clutch at some garment hanging upon the wall, deeming the thing to be an assassin. Mr. Begg says that one day he went out to call upon one Charles Nolin, for the purpose of effecting a reconciliation. While he was sitting in the house eating supper, a man having a gun passed the window; upon which Riel suddenly threw down his knife and fork, and declared that he was about to be shot. Nolin answered that he never would be shot in his house, and immediately went out to see who the man was. It appears that he was an Indian, seeking the way to a comrade's lodge, and perfectly innocent of any murderous intention. Almost immediately after this had occurred, about forty men from the Fort arrived, and accompanied Riel back to his quarters. His terror was so oppressive, that he was threatened with an attack of brain fever.

Sixty miles from Fort Garry was a settlement known as Prairie Portage. The inhabitants to a considerable extent consisted of whitemen, and English and Scotch half-breeds. When news reached this community that the Disturber had taken sixty prisoners and locked them up in Fort Garry, a feeling of the deepest indignation took possession of all. A number of the settlers called upon Major Boulton, a gentleman who had at one time been a captain in the 10th Regiment, and spoke to him in this wise:

"We can muster here 400 good fighting men, and if I you will lead us we shall march against this scoundrel, I liberate the people whom he has shut up in the Fort, and put an end to the rebellion."

"You hold out a very fair prospect," Major Boulton answered, "but I have very grave doubts that the thing can be accomplished as easily as you imagine."

"We have the arms, and we are determined to move against that presumptuous nest of domineering banditti. If you do not lead us, then the command will have to fall upon one of ourselves, and there is no man amongst us who has had any experience in leadership."

"How are your numbers made up?"

"We have nearly a hundred immigrants, and about double that number of English-speaking half-breeds."

"I consent to your request, but you must distinctly know that I do so altogether against my own judgment. Against my *judgment* only, however, not against my inclinations." Very speedily the force was marshalled together, and organised in rough shape. Winter now reigned in all its severity upon the plains. Recently snow had fallen, and without snow shoes it was next to impossible to march. The arms of this crudely-disciplined band, as may be imagined, were not of the most approved pattern. Some of the half-breeds had flint-locks, and their highest average of "going-off" capacity was about 33 1/3 per cent. That is to say, out of three snaps you got the piece "off" once. The miscarriages were made up of "missing fire" and "burning prime."

Now, while this dangerous army was marching toward Fort Garry, Riel, on the advice of his military chief, Lepine, had liberated the prisoners. Many of the latter tarried not long on the shadow of the rebel stronghold. Thomas Scott learned, on leaving the stockade, that a heavy force was proceeding to the Fort to overthrow the rebels, and made all haste to join the loyalists.

Major Boulton was not without some definite and even commendable plan of procedure, much as he has been criticised by those who always show their wisdom *after* the event. To young Scott he detailed his programme.

"My ambition is," he said, "to delude the rebels as to my movements, by affecting a desire to treat with them. Therefore, I shall halt with my forces a short march from Fort Garry, and when I have lulled suspicion, I will make a dash, in the night, trusting to the suddenness and vigour of the onset for success." Such a proceeding Scott strongly approved, and Major Boulton found that the young man's knowledge of the rebels' condition would be of the greatest value to the enterprise. So with considerable enthusiasm the force marched on. Now, however, the sky became a sullen indigo, and flakes of spitting snow began to drive out of the east.

"I have some fear of that sky," the commander said to his followers. "If more snow comes, there is an end of the march." All day, and through the night and during the next day, the storm raged, covering the prairie with four feet of soft snow. Riel's scouts had given warning of the approach of the loyalists, and every man in the fort seized a fire arm, ready to march instantly upon the besiegers. The ruffianly O'Donoghue was fairly in his element.

"Boy hivins and airth," he said, "but it's moyself that's itching to get at those lick-shpittle loyalists. Veeve lah Republeekh," he shouted, tossing his filthy hat, "and God save Oirland."

"We must return, my men," Major Boulton said. "If these well-armed rebels were to come against us now, they would butcher us like sheep." With hearts full of disappointment, the force disbanded, and the men began to retrace their steps homeward. A portion of it, however, remained together. Some in sleighs and others on foot verged off across the prairie from St. John's school-house, in this way endeavouring to avoid Fort Garry. But Riel's eyes had been upon them, and big, unwashed O'Donoghue, mounting his horse, shouted—

"We've got thim. Veeve lah Republeekh; God save Oirland," and set out over the plain, followed by a host of little Frenchmen, bristling like porcupines, with their war-like inclinations.

"Surround the lick-shpittles, Mounsieurs," shouted the big, red Irishman. "Veeve lah, Veeve lah!" he screamed, and beat the flanks of his horse with his monster feet. The big ruffian was fairly delirious for a fight. "Thim are the min. Mounsieurs," he shouted, "that robbed my counthrey of her liberty. Him thim in, Mounsieurs." In this way he continued to shout, his voice sounding over the snowy waste like the bellowing of a bull. As he neared the portage detachment, he perceived Major Boulton, whom he knew.

"Oha," he bellowed, "Mr. Chief Sassenach. Veeve lah Republeekh, God save Oirland! Surrender me brave lick-shpittle. What's this? Tare en nouns, if it isn't Tom Shkott. Divil resaive me you'll not get off this time. Lay down your arms, traitors and crown worshippers. Lay thim down. Drop thim in the shnow. There, don't be too nice. Down wid thim. Or will ye foight? But it's meself that would loike a bit of a shindy wid ye." Thereupon he took his rifle, loaded it, and pointed it at the head of Major Boulton.

"Major," he shouted, "your eye is covered. Divil resaive me if I couldn't knock it out quicker nor you could wink." Then he lowered his piece, waved his greasy hat around his big sorrel head and yelled,

"Veeve lah! Capture thim all, even to that cratur," pointing to a little, thin, spiteful-looking man, with a face much like a weasel's. His skin was the colour of the leaf of the silver poplar, his eyes were very quick, and they snapped and scintillated upon the smallest provocation. He was one of the most cantankerous, self-willed men in the whole company, and was under the impression that his advice was worth the combined wisdom of all the rest. He had heard the contemptuous reference made to himself by O'Donoghue, and his little eyes fairly blazed.

"Yes, me take you also," a big, sodden half-breed said, advancing close to the little man.

"Take me? damn your impertinence! Take me?" and quick as thought itself he drew his pistol and snapped it once, twice, three times in the Metis face. He fairly danced with rage.

"Take me?" he screamed out once again, and, running at the Metis, who had grown alarmed and backed off several paces, he ran the barrel of the pistol down his throat.

"Now, you filthy, red-headed rascal," he said, turning toward the leader, "if you will come down from your horse, I will settle you in the same way," and running over, he stabbed O'Donoghue in the knee with the muzzle of his pistol, and afterwards punched the horse in the ribs. O'Donoghue quickly turned his horse around and, with a sudden movement, squirted a jet of tobacco juice in the eyes of the tempestuous little loyalist.

"Now, take him up to the fort, my min, wid the rest.
Forward, march. Veeve lah Republeekh, and God save Oirland,
Major Boulton," delivering the latter part of the sentence
close to the ear of the captive leader.

[Footnote: The following description of this ridiculous episode in the history of the rebellion is given by Mr. Begg in his history of the troubles:—

"On the morning of the 17th, word was received that the English settlers had disbanded, and were returning to their homes. Soon after this, a small party of men—some in sleighs and others on foot, were seen to verge off across the prairie, from St. John's school-house, appearing as if they wished to avoid the town. As soon as this party was discovered, a body of horsemen emerged from Fort Garry, and started out for the purpose of intercepting them. People in the town, crowded every available spot overlooking the prairie. Faces thronged the windows. Wood piles and fences were crowded with sightseers, all expecting to behold a miniature battle. When the Portage party discovered the French coming out of the Fort they halted, and appeared to hold a consultation; after which, they moved slowly on—the depth of snow impeding their progress. The French, at the head of whom was O'Donoghue, continued to gallop over the snow drifts, halting now and again for stragglers. At last the two parties met, but instead of a fight, they mixed together for some minutes, and then they all started in the direction of Fort Garry. They have been taken prisoners, was the conclusion by the lookers-on, and so, indeed, it turned out to be. Several of the Portage party refused at first to give up their arms; but ultimately they consented to do so, and were all taken to Fort Garry, where they were imprisoned in the same rooms which had only recently been vacated by the first lot of prisoners. It is said that the Portage party gave themselves up, on the understanding that Riel merely wished to speak to them and explain matters. If this is the case, they were not justly dealt by, for immediately upon their arrival at Fort Garry, they were put in prison, and Major Boulton, their leader, placed in irons. What a singular change in affairs this occasioned;—twenty-four prisoners liberated on the 15th,—forty-eight prisoners taken on the 17th."]

Let us now return to the vengeful Riel. Never steady of purpose, or resting his faith upon logic, he had begun to curse himself for taking Lepine's advice and suffering Scott to depart.

"After all, he may elude me, go out of the territory, and marry the girl. Curses, a thousand curses upon my own head for following the advice. Malediction upon Lepine's head for having given it to me." Just at this moment, the door opened, and Lepine entered.

"I bring Monsieur good news."

"Ah, what is it? Any tidings of Scott?"

"He is at this very moment in the fort; having been caught among Major Boulton's party. He was most insolent to myself and O'Donoghue, and used very abusive language respecting yourself. I think, Monsieur, you have cause sufficient against him now."

"Bon! bon! Yes,—he shall not escape me this time," and rising, he began to stride up and down the floor, his eyes flaming with hate and vengeance.

"Now, Monsieur Lepine, give me your attention. At once go and put Boulton in irons. I shall attend presently, and declare that he is to be shot to-morrow. Suppliants will come beseeching me to spare his life, but at first I will refuse to do so, and say that I am determined to carry out my threat. At the last I will yield. So far, so good. I do not know, now, whether you understand my methods or not."

[Footnote: The following is Mr. Begg's version of this part of the affair:— "Riel granted the lives of three, but Major Boulton, he said, would have to die that night. It now began to look very serious. Archdeacon McLean was called upon to attend the condemned man during his last moments, and a feeling of oppression was felt by all at the thought of a human being to be thus sent to his last account on such short notice, at midnight, too (the hour appointed for the execution)—midnight—the very thought of a man being brought out in the stillness of the night to be shot like a dog was horrible in the extreme. Still there were no lack of interceders, although little hope was now entertained of Major Boulton being spared. People retired to their homes that evening with mingled feelings of hope and Uncertainty, mixed with horror at the deed about to be committed. And how was the prisoner during all this time? Calm and resigned to his fate. After writing a few lines to his friends in Canada, he called for a basin of water and a towel with which to wash his face and hands, and a glass of wine to prevent him, if possible, from shivering when passing into the cold night air, in case people might attribute it to fear. He spoke quietly and calmly of the fate before him, and acted altogether as a soldier should do in the face of death. In the meantime the French councillors were sitting in deliberation on Boulton's sentence, the result being that his life was spared. This was communicated at once to the prisoner who received the information as calmly as he had done the sentence of death."]

"I think I do Monsieur," and there was a knowing twinkle in the eye of the wily scoundrel.

"Well, this Scott has an unbridled tongue, and is pretty certain to use it. If he does not, a little judicious goading will soon set him in his most abusive mood. If possible, it would be well for one of the guards to provoke him to commit an assault. Could you rely upon any one of your men for such a bit of business?"

"Oui, Monsieur, I have such a man."

"Bon, let him be so provoked, and after his violence has been thoroughly trumpeted through the fort, make a declaration of the same formally to me. I will then direct you to try him by court martial. You are aware of how I desire him to be disposed of. When the news gets abroad that he is to be shot, some will be incredulous, and others will come to sue for his life. I shall reply to them: 'This is a matter of discipline. The man has deserved death, or the court martial would not have sentenced him. I spared Boulton's life, and already I have as fruits of my leniency, increased turbulence and disrespect. The government of this colony must be respected, and the only way to teach its enemies that it must be, is to make an example of one of the greatest offenders.' Lose no time in completing the work. We know not what chance may work, and rob our hands of the scoundrel. You understand? I am least of all mixed up in the matter, being more concerned with weightier affairs."

"Oui, Monsieur," and making an obeisance, the murderous tool departed. Exactly as it had been planned, it all fell out. Major Boulton was put in irons, and Riel declared that for the sake of peace and the prosperity of the colony, he must be shot. Dozens of people came and implored him to spare the condemned man's life; but he was inexorable. At last, however, "at the eleventh hour," as the newspapers put it, yielding to Mr. Donald A. Smith he said:

"He is spared."

Lepine presented himself before his leader.

"Monsieur, I think that it will not be at all necessary to employ any stratagem to work our man into violence. He has been showering reproaches upon the guards, and loading your name with every sort of ignominious reproach. The guards knew my feelings respecting the man, so during the night they decided to put chains upon him. As the foremost one advanced with the manacles, the prisoner raised his arm, and dealt him a blow on the head which felled him to the ground."

"Bon! Bon!" Riel cried, while he rubbed his hands with satisfaction. "Without applying the little goad at all, he fulfils our will."

"Well, not in the strictest sense, Monsieur. Luc had certain private instructions from me, and he carried them out in a very skilful manner."

"N'importe, Monsieur, N'importe how the thing came about; we have the cause against him, and that suffices. What do you now propose to do, for you are aware Monsieur—" there was now a tone of diabolical raillery in his words—" that this is a matter in which I cannot concern myself, you being the best judge of what is due rebellious military prisoners?"

"Merci, Monsieur! I shall endeavour to merit your further regard. My intention is to proceed forthwith to try him. Already, I have summoned the witnesses of his guilt; and he and you shall know our decision before another hour has passed." Then the faithful Monsieur Lepine was gone.

"No, ma Marie. You shall never deck your nuptial chamber with daisies for Monsieur Thomas Scott. You will find occupation for your sweet little fingers in putting fresh roses upon the mound that covers him. For a *feu-de-joie* and the peal of glad marriage bells, I will give you, ma petite chere, the sullen toll that calls him to his open coffin, and the rattle of musketry that stills the tongue which uttered to you the last love pledge."

For an hour did he pace up and down the floor gloating over his revenge. Meanwhile I shall leave him, and follow the "adjutant-general," as M. Lepine was known under the Provisional Government. He proceeded to the private room of the military quarters, and entering found his subordinate officers assembled there.

"Messieurs," he said, "We know what our business is. We must lose no time in dispatching it. But before commencing, let me say a few words. Monsieur Riel is so overweighted with other affairs that the matter of dealing with the man Scott rests entirely in our hands. I have just left him, after endeavouring in vain to induce him to be present at the trial; but he could not spare the time to come. By skilfully sounding him, however, I discovered that his sentiment respecting the prisoner are exactly the same as those entertained by myself. What these are, I need hardly say. It is now a struggle between the authority of the Provisional Government and a horde of rebellious persons of which the defendant is the most dangerous. The eyes of our followers are upon us; and if we permit the authority of government to be defied, its officers reviled, and insult heaped upon us, depend upon it we shall speedily lose the hold which we have gained after so many bitter struggles; and become ridiculous, and a prey to the conspiracy which our enemies are so actively engaged in promoting against us. The very fact of this man Scott having leagued himself with our enemies, within a few hours after his release from confinement, is in itself an offence worthy of death; but I shall ask these persons who are here as witnesses to show you that since his capture he has merited death ten times over at our hands. With your permission gentlemen, I will proceed:

"Thomas Scott of Red River Settlement stands charged before this court-martial with treasonable revolt against the peace and welfare of the colony; with having leagued himself with an armed party, whose object was the overthrow of authority as vested in our Provisional Government. He is likewise charged with having attempted criminal violence upon lawfully delegated guards appointed over him, during his incarceration; and likewise with inciting his fellow-prisoners to insubordination and tumult, contrary to the order and well being of authority as established in Red River."

"Luc Lestang."

This person came forward.

"Relate all you know in the conduct of the prisoner Scott that may be regarded as treasonable and criminal, within the past fourteen days."

"On the 17th ultimo, I was present at his capture, a short distance from Fort Garry. He was armed, and was in company with a number of other armed persons who had leagued themselves under one Major Boulton, with the object of capturing Fort Garry, and overthrowing the Provisional Government as established in this colony."

"Have you seen him since his imprisonment in the Fort?"

"I have seen him every day since."

"Will you please state what have been his demeanour and conduct as a prisoner?"

"He has been insulting and disorderly in the last degree."

"Will you specify a few particular examples?"

"I have frequently heard him describe the Provisional Government and its supporters as a band of mongrel rough-scruffs, a greasy, insolent, nest of traitors; and a lot of looting, riotous, unwashed savages. He has used language of this sort ever since his entry into the Fort. Likewise, I have heard him say, that he would have the pleasure of assisting in hanging Monsieur Riel to a prairie poplar; and in putting tar and feathers upon his unwashed, hungry followers."

"Has he been guilty of any acts of violence?"

"He has been guilty of acts of violence. When he became unbearably insubordinate I found it to be my duty to put irons upon him. As I approached him with the handcuffs he smote me twice in the face, and I yet carry the mark that he gave me. [Here the precious half-breed pointed to his right eye, which was a dusky purple.] This black eye I received from one of his blows."

"That will do, Luc."

Another witness with the movements of a snake, and eyes as black as sloes, was called; and he gave evidence which tallied exactly with that sworn to by Luc Lestang. This, of course, was not a very extraordinary coincidence, for he had been present while the first miscreant was giving his evidence. But poor Scott, whose life was the issue of all the swearing, was not permitted to be present, but was kept without in a distant room, chained there like a wild beast.

"The Court," said the adjutant-general, "has heard the accusation against this man; and its duty now is to consider whether or not the safety, the peace, the well-being of the government and the state, demands that the extreme penalty should be visited upon this common disturber and enemy both. The question is, whether he is worthy of Death, or not. You will retire gentlemen,—" there were four of them, exclusive of witnesses, and the clerk—"and find your verdict."

They were absent about two minutes. The foreman then advancing said:

"Monsieur Adjutant, WE FIND THE PRISONER SCOTT, GUILTY."

Then drawing upon his head a black cap, the adjutant said:

"After due and deliberate trial by this Court, it has been found that the prisoner Thomas Scott, is 'Guilty.' *I do, therefore, declare the sentence of this court martial to be, that the prisoner be taken forth this day, at one o'clock, and shot.* And may God in His infinite mercy, have mercy upon his soul."

Monsieur Riel had been all this while pacing up and down his room. A tap came upon his door.

"Entrez. Ah, it is you, mon adjutant!"

"Oui, mon president."

"What tidings?"

"C'est accompli. The court-martial has found the prisoner guilty; and he is condemned to be shot at one o'clock this day."

"Monsieur is expeditious! Monsieur is zealous. C'est bon, c'est bon; merci, Monsieur." And the miscreant walked about delirious with the exuberance of his gratification. Then he came over to where his adjutant stood, and shook his hand; then he thrust his fingers through his hair, and half bellowed, his voice resembling that of some foul beast.

"La patrie has reason to be proud of her zealous son," and he again shook the hand of his infamous lieutenant. Then with a very low bow M. Lepine left the room, saying as he departed,

"I shall endeavour to merit to the fullest the kindly eulogy which Monsieur President bestows upon me." The news of Scott's sentence spread like fire around the settlement. Some believed that the penalty would not be carried out, while others declared that they thought otherwise.

"If this prisoner is pardoned, people will begin to treat the sentences of the Provisional Authorities as good jokes. Riel must be aware of this; therefore Scott is likely to suffer the full penalty." Several persons called upon the tyrant, and besought him to extend mercy to the condemned man, but he merely shrugged his shoulders!

"This prisoner has been twice rebellious. He has set bad example among the prisoners, assaulted his keeper, and loaded the Provisional Government with opprobrium. I may say to you, Messieurs, however, that I have really nothing to do with the man's case. In this time of tumult, when the operation of all laws is suspended, the Court-Martial is the only tribunal to which serious offenders can be referred. This young man, Scott, has had fair trial, as fair as a British Court-Martial would have given him, and he has been sentenced to death. I assume that he would not have received such a sentence if he had not deserved it. Therefore I shall not interfere. There is no use, Messieurs, in pressing me upon the matter. At heart, I shall grieve as much as you to see the young man cut off, but his death I believe necessary now, as an example to the hundreds who are desirous of overthrowing the authority, which we have established in the colony." The petitioners left the tyrant with sorrowful faces.

"My God!" one of them exclaimed, "it is frightful to murder this young man, whose only offence is resistance to probable insult from his debased, half-breed keeper. Is there nothing to be done?"

No, there was nothing to be done. The greasy, vindictive tyrant was lord and master of the situation When Riel was alone, he began once more to walk up and down the room, and thus mused aloud:

"I shall go down to his cell. Perhaps, if I pretend that
I will spare his life, he may tell me where resides Marie.

"Yes," he was sure that he would succeed, "I shall get his secret by promising pardon; then I will spit upon his face and say 'die dog, I'll not spare you.'" So forth he sallied, and made his way to the cell where the young man sat in chains.

"Well, malignant tyrant, what do you here? Whatever your business is, let it be dispatched quickly, for your presence stifles me. What dishonourable proposal have you now to make?"

"Monsieur Scott, it seems to be a positive pleasure to you to revile me. Yet have I sought to serve you;—Yea, I would have been, would now be, your friend."

"Peace; let me hear what it is that you now propose?"

"You are aware that it is ordered by Court-Martial, of which, I was not a member, that you are to be shot at one o'clock this day? It is now just forty-five minutes of one. I can spare your life, and I will do it, upon one condition."

"Pray let me hear what dishonour it is that you propose? I ask the question now, for the same reason that I made a similar query during my first incarceration, out of a curiosity to learn, if possible, a little more of your meanness and infamy."

"And I reply to you as I answered before, that I shall
take no notice of your revilings, but make my proposal.
I simply ask you to state to me where Jean and his daughter
Marie have taken up their abode?"

"Where you will never find them. That's my answer, villain and tyrant, and now begone."

"Perhaps you imagine that the sentence will not be carried out. I ask you to choose between life and liberty, and an almost immediate ignominious death."

"I care not for your revenge, or your mercy. Once more I say, get you gone." Then the ruffian turned round, rushed at the chained prisoner, and dealt him a terrific kick in the side, after which he spat upon his face.

"She shall be mine!" he hissed, "when your corpse lies mouldering in a dishonoured traitor's grave." The young man was chained to a heavy table, but with a sudden wrench, he freed himself, raised both arms, and was about bringing down his manacled hands upon the tyrant miscreant —and that blow would have ended the rebellion at Red River,—when Luc burst into the room, seized the prisoner, and threw him. While his brute knee was on the young man's breast, and his greasy hand held the victim's throat, Riel made his escape, and turned back to his own quarters.

As for poor Scott, when the tyrant, and the brutal guard had left the cell, he began to pace up and down, sorely disturbed. All along he had cherished the hope that the tyrant would be induced to commute the sentence to lengthy imprisonment. But the diabolical vengeance which he had seen in the tyrant's eye now began to undermine his hope of life. Some friends were admitted to his cell, and they informed him that they had pleaded for him, but in vain.

"And do you think that he will really perpetrate this murderous deed?" he asked.

"Most assuredly he will; and now nothing remains for you but to prepare to meet your doom like a true man. You are not the first who has suffered in like manner in a cause which history will ever associate with your name. The tyrant who prevails over you, will not triumph for long. Ignominious will be the atonement that he must pay. But you have to show that for the sacred cause of loyalty you know *how* to die. You have made your peace with God, and there is nought then that you have to fear. You sorrow at going alone, leaving all the world after you, but we go hence too, in a little; and every hour the clock tells, yields a thousand souls to eternity."

"Ah, my friends, this is all true, but I am young, and
I had cherished one very sweet hope."

"This has been the fate of tens of thousands."

"I should not have shrunk from death six months ago, had he set me up as a target for his half-breed murderers. I should have uttered no word of repining, but it is different now: O God, it is very different."

All hung down their heads. They were vainly trying to hide their tears.

"And even for myself, under the new condition which has arisen, I would not care. It is because of *her*—because of my pure, beautiful love, my Marie, whom this fiend has so persecuted, that I cannot look upon my doom with calmness. I had thought that there was such a happy future in store for us, for her and me, when this tumult was ended!" Then he took paper and pen and wrote a letter, which, when he had sealed it, he gave into the hands of the clergyman.

"That address must be known only to one," he said. "It is not safe to post the letter anywhere in Canada; but, as a dying request, I ask that you have it put in the post at Pembina."

"I shall with my own hand deliver it. I shall set out to-morrow."

"May God, sir, send you comfort in your affliction. Pray remain as long as you can with my darling;—tell her, for it will help her better to bear the blow, that I was cheerful, and that I said I had no fear but that she and I would meet it heaven, and that when I went there I would pray to my God in her behalf every day. She has no token of mine. Take this ring and give it to her, and my scarf-pin, which in her sweet, childish fancy she used so to admire. Tell her that I died—I have told her in my letter—but repeat it to her, with my heart full, O so full! of love for her."

There was now a rude bustling at the door; the rusty key was plied, and with a harsh scream the bolt flew back. Then the evil-looking Luc entered, followed by five or six others, all of whom were partially intoxicated.

"Your hour has come, young man," he said, in a brutal voice. "Let us be going."

"My God, this is a cold-blooded murder," poor Scott said, turning to Mr. Donald A. Smith and the Rev. Mr. Young. Then he bade good-bye to the visitors and to his fellow prisoners, and walked forth with the guard closely accompanied by Mr. Young. Before they got outside the prison door the miscreant leader said,

"Stop a moment." Then taking a white handkerchief he tied it round the victim's eyes. Regarding it for a moment, he said, "That will do, I guess. Here, two of you men, take him by the arms." During this time the prisoner was engaged in deep prayer, and remained so till he reached the place of execution. This was a few yards distant, upon the snow, where a coffin had been placed to receive his body. Addressing Mr. Young, he said:

"Shall I stand or kneel?"

"Kneel," the clergyman answered in a low voice.

"Farewell," [Footnote: I get the details of the execution from a report of the occurrence by Hon. Donald A. Smith. The extract is likewise to be found in Captain Huyshe's Bed River Expedition, pp. 18-19.—The Author.] he said, to Mr. Young, then "My poor Marie!" While these words were upon his lips there were several rifle reports, and this high-spirited, sunny-hearted young fellow, fell backwards into his coffin, pierced by three bullets. Mr. Young returned to the body but found the victim was still alive. He groaned several times and moved his hands; whereupon one of the party approached with a pistol and discharged it into the sufferer's face. The bullet entered at the eye and passed round the head. Then the body was straightened out in the coffin and the lid nailed down. The whole affair was so revoltingly cruel that it is with pain one is obliged to write about it. It is said, and upon authority that there is little room to question, that even after the cover had been put upon the coffin, the young man was still heard to groan, and even to cry. Mr. Young then asked that he might be permitted to take the body and give it interment in the burying ground of the

Presbyterian Congregation, but his request was not granted, and a similar favour was refused to the Bishop of Rupert's Land. The body was taken inside the Fort where Lepine declared it was to be buried; and where an actual burial did take place before a number of spectators. The coffin, afterwards exhumed, was found to contain only stones and rubbish. What the fate of the body was no one has since discovered, but it has been conjectured that it was taken during the night by Riel's bloodhounds and dropped through the ice into the river.

Mr. Young was faithful to his pledge. On the following day he set out over the bitter, snowy wastes for Pembina, and thence through storm, and over pathless stretches he held his way till he reached the settlement where abode Marie and her father.

She was sitting at the window-pane thinking of her lover when the stranger passed; and she opened the door to the clergyman's knock. There could be no mistaking who this girl was, and the clergyman's heart was numb as he looked upon her.

"Did he send me any message?" And then reflecting that this man was a stranger who may never have seen her lover, she blushed deeply. But she recovered herself in a moment.

"Where does Monsieur come from?"

"From Winnipeg."

"O, then," she thought, "he perhaps *does* know my beloved. Is there peace there now," she asked, "or is that wicked man still at his evil deeds?"

"There is not peace at Red River, my child. Come in;—it is to speak to you about events at Red River that I have come all the way from that far settlement."

She learnt her doom, and the good clergyman sat by her trying to afford some consolation. But she seemed not to understand the meaning of his words, or even to hear them. The blow had been too overwhelming for mortal tongue to fashion words that could convey aught of comfort. She sat there, her face like a stone, her eyes tearless. Yes, she read his letter and kissed his presents. She would fold the letter sometimes and lay it away near to her heart. Then she would open it again, spread it upon her lap, and sit half the day alternately looking at, and tenderly handling it. A few days and nights were spent during which she spake no word, eat no food, nor took any sleep. At the end of the fourth day they found her on a little seat beside the door where *he* had said good-bye to her. She had his letter in her hand and his ring upon her finger. But she was dead.

CHAPTER IX.

After the return of Mr. McDougall to Ottawa, and while the Government press busied itself in laying upon that gentleman's shoulders the blame which should have been debited to the blundering of the administration, steps were being taken to have an armed force sent at once to the scene of tumult, to restore the authority of the Queen. Sir Garnet Wolseley, who has since earned distinction in bush and desert fighting, was the officer put in charge of the expedition.

Before this step had been taken, however, the government had set the wheels of a totally different sort of force in motion. Monseigneur Tache, to whom I have already referred, was absent in Rome attending the Ecumenical Council, when the disturbance broke out. Sir John went to M. George E. Cartier then, and said:

"My idea is that the man who can do more to settle this matter than all the wisdom of the Government combined, is Monseigneur Tache. What think you—would it not be well to represent the case to him by cable, and ask him to return?"

"Oui, Sir John,—the suggestion is good." So the bishop was cabled for, and he came home. "Well, Messieurs," he said, "what function is it with which you would endow me? With what have I to deal?"

"The people are in open, armed rebellion. They do not want to come into the confederation; and there is an extensive desire for annexation. The head of the movement is Louis Riel, and he is president of the Provisional Government. He has seized and invested Fort Garry, set up laws for himself, and is feeding and supplying his troops with the property of the Hudson's Bay Company." [Let it be borne in mind that, at this time, the murder of Scott had not been committed, and Riel and his followers were only known to be guilty of having risen in armed revolt, and consumed much of the stores of the Hudson's Bay Company].

"Well, Messieurs, the case is made plain. Now, with what authority do you endow me?"

"We authorize you to say to the Rebels, on behalf of the Government, that if they will peaceably depart to their homes, and submit to the authority of the Queen, as represented by the Government of Canada, no harm will come to them. We authorize you further, to assure them that the Government will stand between them and the Hudson's Bay Company, should the latter seek recompense for stores consumed, or property appropriated. Finally, for the offences committed—and which we have specified —you shall, on our behalf, extend pardon to each and all."

Armed with this authority, the bishop set out. Before he reached Winnipeg the blood-thirsty president had murdered Scott. I hope the reader has not forgotten that Monseigneur was the same divine who used to look with delight upon Louis Riel when a child, and stroke his glossy, black hair. That he was the same gentleman who found for the lad a benefactress in the person of Madame Masson.

The stars were fighting for the murderer, and he knew it when he heard that his personal friend and warm admirer was coming. His Lordship was not nearly as badly shocked as most humane people might suppose, when he heard that Thomas Scott had been butchered like a dog upon the snow. Indeed, there is some authority to say that he was not shocked at all. His good priest, Pere Richot, who got the bishop's ear, took a highly moral and humane view of the matter.

"Shooting served the fellow right, Monseigneur," [Footnote: Captain Huyshe and several other writers of high repute, are my authority for this statement.] he said. "He was a disturber, and it was good to make an example of him."

In a little, we may be sure, the Monseigneur's opinion did not differ very widely from that of the "crocmitaine" priest.

"Let the people all assemble," the bishop proclaimed: "I have important declarations to make to them." They obeyed his mandate, and he said:

"I am authorized by the Government of Canada, to inform you that if you forthwith depart to your lawful habitations in peace, you will have nothing to fear. Your rebellious deeds will be forgiven to you; the other unfortunate event will likewise be overlooked, and the Hudson Bay Company, whose provisions you have eaten and whose property you have appropriated, will be indemnified by government, if they take steps to obtain restitution for the same."

One month later, years afterwards, this precious divine maintained that the authority with which he had been clothed by the Government—and I have given that authority *substantially*—endowed him with the power to grant pardon for the murder of Scott! Without tiring the reader, let me say that it was by means of the discussion and the perplexities which subsequently arose upon this point, that the miscreant-fiend escaped the vengeance of the law. *Monseigneur had not lost his interest or affection yet for the lad for whom he had procured an education!*

The bloody Guiteau, however, did not consider the pardon a very great act of liberality. On the contrary, he was inclined to regard the discussion of his guilt, the guilt of the president of an independent colony! who was law-maker and law-dispenser in himself, as somewhat of an impertinence. He still continued to administer the government, and to live sumptuously in the house of Governor McTavish. About him here he had gathered some of his most powerful followers, one of which was the big fenian, O'Donoghue. These ate and drank to their heart's content, but from their wallowing and disgusting habits the residence soon resembled a filthy lair where pigs lie down. Yet the Rebel Chief had spared no pains to make it luxurious; conveying thither, with other plunder, the effects of the house of Dr. Schultz.

When it was at first told Riel that Sir Garnet Wolseley, at the head of a large force, was marching against him, he refused to believe it. It was not till he actually with his own eyes, saw the troops that he was convinced. Then with hysterical precipitation the greasy murderer scurried out of the Fort, mounted a horse, and rode away in mortal terror. Later, he was reduced to the necessity of walking, and when his boots were worn off his feet, there was blood in his foot-prints. In this plight he met a follower who used to tremble before him in the days of his power, and to be like unto Caius Marius, he said to this man:

"Go back and tell your friends that you have met Louis Riel, a fugitive, barefooted, without a roof above his head, and no where to go." This beastly, murderous tyrant did actually imagine himself to be a hero!

Later on he was supplied with money by Sir John Macdonald to keep out of the country. The amount was not paid to him in a lump, but his good friend, the whilome bishop, and now archbishop, paid it out whenever the worthless, vagabond rascal came and represented himself as being very needy.

He often, in his fallen days, would go about sighing for Marie, and declaring that, with all his vengeful feelings towards her, she was the only maiden whom he had ever really loved. Old Jean came back and settled with a sad heart, in the little cottage where had grown up his sweet Marie. It was very desolate for his old heart now. The ivy wreathed itself about the little wicker house, as was its wont, but Marie was not there. The cows came as usual to the bars to be milked, but there was a lamenting in their lowing call. They missed the small, soft hand that used to milk them, and never more heard the blithe, glad voice singing from *La Claire Fontaine.* Paul worked bravely and strove to cheer his father;

and Violette, with her bright, quick eyes, just a little like Marie's, would come down and sing to him, and bring him cool, pink, dew-bathed roses. He thanked them all; but their love was not sufficient. His heart was across the prairies by a grave upon which the violets were growing. Before the leaves fell he was lying by her side. A cypress marks the graves, and the little brook goes by all the summer.

CHAPTER X.

We left the murderer upon the plains making speeches like Marius on the ruins of Carthage. The self-imposed banishment did not endure for long; and the swarthy face of Louis Riel was once more seen in Riviere Rouge. When tidings of the murder got abroad, English-speaking Canada cried out that the felon should be handed over to justice. I say English-speaking Canada, for the French people almost to a man gave their sympathy to the man whose hands were red with the blood of his fellow creature. They could not be induced to look upon the slaying as an act of inhuman, bloody, ferocity, with which the question of race or religion had not the remotest connection.

"It is because Riel, a Frenchman and a Roman Catholic, shot Thomas Scott, an Englishman and a Protestant, that all this crying for vengeance is heard over the land. Now, had the cases been reversed, we would hear no English lamentings over a murdered Riel." This was in effect what they said, impossible, almost, as it might seem for one to be able to credit it. For illiterate persons, who could see no treason in the uprising, to condone the tumult and havoc, and regard even the murder justifiable, was what might have been expected. But what shall be said for M. George E. Cartier, the "enlightened statesman," for Pere Richot, the "crocmitaine," for Pere Lastanc, the Vicar-General, and finally, for Monseigneur himself? Nothing can be said! We can only as Canadians all hang down our heads in shame, that any section of our common country should make such an exhibition of itself in the sight of humanity.

The protege of the Hierarchy was not long to mope about the plains like another dumb and fallen Saturn. No less proportions than that of un Dieu hors de combat, a very God overthrown, would the deluded followers accord to the overwhelmed chief. The clergy never suffered any aspersion to be thrown upon "le grand homme" for by no less appellation was he known.

"He has been your benefactor," the coarse "crocmitaine" Richot would say. "Had he not risen and compelled Government to grant you your rights, you would forever have been down-trodden by Canadian tyrants. When the rage of the heretics in Ontario shall have cooled down we must send Le Bienfaiteur to Parliament. And the time did actually come when the murderer appeared upon the hustings in the West soliciting the votes of the people. Nor did he appeal in vain. *He was elected.* Nay, more than this, he set out for Ottawa, entered that city, and in the open light of day walked up to the Parliament Buildings, and in the eyes of officials and of the public subscribed his name to the Members' roll. Thousands have been in the habit of denouncing Sir John for permitting an unhung felon to go about as a free man, but when he came red-handed and presuming to Ottawa and enrolled his name, the Reformers were in power."

Before this date, however, the criminal had secured some official eulogy in the West. And it happened in this wise. Some time after the appointment of Mr. Archibald to the Lieutenant-Governorship of Manitoba, several bands of Fenians threatened to invade the territory, and set up above the plains a green flag with a harp and a shamrock upon it. Mr. Archibald had at hand no force to resist the threatened attack, and he became almost delirious with alarm. So he sent a messenger to M. Riel, the untried felon, whose crime was at the time the subject of voluminous correspondence between Canada and the Colonial Office, accepting a proposal made by the ex-Rebel to call out the half-breeds in defence of the new Province. The Fenians did not carry out their threat, but it was much the same for the murderer of poor Scott as if they had. When the danger was blown over the Lieutenant-Governor walked in front of the ex-Rebel lines, expressed his gratitude to the men, and warmly shook hands with Riel and Lepine.

The presence of Riel was yet a standing menace to peace among the half-breeds beyond the limits of the new province. The Canadian Government began to devise means of getting him out of the country. They tried persuasion, but this was not an effective mode. It was at this juncture that a sum was put into the hands of Archbishop Tache to pay the felon in consideration of his withdrawal. All this time Ontario was crying out for the capture of the man; and it was while the amount was being placed to the murderer's credit with the Archbishop, that Sir John raised his eyes toward heaven and said:

"I wish to God I could catch him!"

So Riel took himself out of Canada, and traversed American territory till he found a district it Montana, thickly inhabited by half-breeds. Here he established himself in a sort of a fashion, sometimes tilling the soil, frequently hunting, but all the while talking about Red River. He soon began to forget Marie, and to cast languishing eyes upon some of the half-breed girls living upon the airy uplands. [Footnote: It is stated upon certain authority, how good I don't know, that the brave M. Riel rejoices in the possession of three wives. One is said to be a French Metis, the other a Scotch half-breed, and the third a beautiful Cree squaw with large dusky eyes.] He was regarded as a great hero by these maidens, for long before his coming the daring, brilliancy, and great achievements of Monsieur Riel had been told with enthusiasm at the fireside of every half-breed in Montana. We shall leave M. Riel in Montana, sometimes working, sometimes hunting, always wooing, and take a very brief glance at the causes which led up to the present outbreak.

Under the new legislation for the territories, only those half-breeds within the bounds of the new province were guaranteed secure possession of their land. Under the principle that all territory not granted in specific form to individuals by the Ministers of the Crown, is the property of the Crown, each half-breed who occupied a lot of land under the Hudson Bay Company's rule, was regarded as a squatter under the new regime. To make such holding valid, therefore, the Government issued patents to *bona fide* squatters, who then found themselves on the same footing as the white immigrants. But beyond Manitoba, and chiefly in Prince Albert, there were large numbers of half-breeds settled over the prairie. So long as no immigrant came prying about for choice land the half-breeds had naught to complain about, but the rapid influx of population soon altered the whole face of the matter. Several squatters who had toiled for many a long year upon holdings, were obliged to make way for strangers who had "friends at court"—for even in the North West wilderness there is, in this sense, a court—and who took a fancy to the particular piece of land upon which "these lazy half-breeds" were squatting. Newspapers, whose business it is to keep the skirts of government clean in the matter, deny this altogether. But, unfortunately, there is no use in denying it. It is but too true, and it is with a feeling of very great regret that I myself, a Conservative, and a warm well-wisher of the administration, affirm it. It is true that in many and many a case, in a greater number of instances than even opponents of the administration suppose, a half-breed who has toiled for a number of years upon a lot, effecting improvements and taking pride in his property, has been dispossessed by an incomer because he could not show a patent from the Interior Department.

But almost as fruitful a source of dissatisfaction as these heartless and dishonest displacements has been the difficulty which the unfortunate squatter has experienced in obtaining his patent. The mills of the gods in the Interior Department grind very slowly. The obtaining of a patent by a deserving squatter as a general rule is about as difficult, and as worthy of applause when achieved, as is the task which lies before a farmer's boy who has decided to become a member of parliament, by first earning money enough to go to school to prepare for a third class teachership, by then teaching school till he has a sufficient competency to study medicine, and by then practising his profession till he finds himself able to capture the riding. Of course there is some excuse, and we must not forget to produce it, for the Department of the Interior. It would be undignified if it were to move with any degree of rapidity. According to etiquette, and the rule is very proper, when the application of the half-breed comes to the office, it must remain for at least four weeks in the drawer set apart for "correspondence to be read." After it has been read it receives one or two marks with a red-lead pencil, after which it is deposited in pigeon-hole No. 1. Now no document ever lodges for a shorter time than a month in pigeon-hole No. 1; and if at the end of that period it should happen to be removed, the clerk lays by his novel or tooth-pick, as the case may be, and puts one or two blue marks upon the back of it. When we consider that there are all the way from six to twenty pigeon-holes, by a simple process of arithmetic we can get approximately near the period which it takes the poor half-breed's prayer to get from pigeon-hole Alpha to pigeon-hole Omega. But during the process the back of the squatter's application has become a work of art. It is simply delightful to look upon. It not alone contains memoranda and hieroglyphics made in red and blue pen-pencil but it is also beautified by marks made upon it in carmine ink, in ink "la brillanza," an azure blue ink, in myrtle green ink, in violette noire; but never, it must be said to the credit of the department, in common black. But all these colours are worthless indeed, viewed from any point of view, compared with its other acquisitions. Solomon himself in all his glory was never decked out more gorgeously than this poor half-breed's greasy sheet of foolscap is at the end of its journey through the pigeon-holes. The prime minister of the Crown in all his pomp of imperial orders has not so many ribbons as this poor vagabond's claim. Sometimes it is swathed in crimson tyings, sometimes in scarlet, now and again in magenta; and I am very happy to be able to say that pink and two very exquisite shades of blue known as birds-egg and cobalt have lately been introduced.

Of course the half-breed complains when the weeks have swelled into months, and the months have got out of their teens, that he has heard no answer to his prayer; but the rascal should try to consider that his document has to make its voyage through the pigeon holes.

In this way there has been much heartburning, and many curses against officialdom and red-tape. While the back of the application is being turned out a christmas card, a stray immigrant comes along, and the squatter half-breed has once more to go back for a new camping-ground.

But there is something to be said—this time I am serious—for the Department in the matter, though not a very great deal. A number of the half-breeds, though a small, a very, very small proportion of the whole, are restless vagabonds, who squat upon lands with no intention of remaining permanently, but only with the object of speculation by selling their scrip, leaving the neighbourhood, taking up another lot, and receiving in like manner disposable scrip again. But the officers of the North-West must know that the half-breed people, *in general*, are constant-working, and are desirous of achieving comfort, and of affluence. Yet because of the acts of a few unprincipled, lazy wanderers, some will seek to convey the impression that the conduct of the small few is a type of the methods of all.

There is still, among the many irritating causes, all of which my limits will not permit me to dwell upon, one which must not go unnoticed. Mr. Dewdney is not the gentleman who ought to have the immediate administration of North-West affairs in his hands. He has neither the understanding nor the inclination to make him a suitable administrator. Before all things he is there for himself; and he has even figured in the respectable role of land-grabbing. I am sure that if the gentleman is to be provided for by the public no objection would be raised if Sir John were to propose that he be recalled, and receive his salary all the same in consideration of the position he holds in the regard of the prime-minister, and of those who are not exactly prime-ministers or ministers. Mr. Dewdney has not alone got it into his head that an Indian has no understanding; but he must also endow himself with the conviction that he has no nostrils. A friend of Mr. Dewdney got some meat, but the article stank, and the importer knew not how to dispose of it.

"O sell it to the Indians," the Governor said; and, "Lo! to the poor Indian" it was sold; and sold at tenderloin prices.

"We can't eat em meat. He stinks," the poor savage said.
"Em charge too much. Meat very bad."

"Let Indians eat their meat," the just Mr. Dewdney retorted; "or starve and be damned." What right has an Indian to complain of foul meat, and to say that he has been charged too high a price for it? He is only a savage!

Let Sir John take care.

Well, this was the state of affairs when Louis Riel, about a year ago, left off his wooing for a little while, and returned to the old theatre of his crimes. He found the people chafing under official injustice, and delays that were almost equivalent to a denial of justice. He did not care a fig for the condition of "his people!" but like the long-winged petrel, he is a bad weather bird, and here was his opportunity. He went abroad among the people, fomenting the discord, and assuring them that if all other means failed they would obtain their rights by rising against the authorities.

But the plain object of this plausible disturber was cash. The lazy rascal had failed to earn a livelihood among the half-breeds of Montana; and now was resolved to get some help from the Dominion Treasury. Presently intimations began to reach the Canadian Government that if they made it worth M. Riel's while, he would leave the disaffected people and return to American territory. The sum of $5,000, it was learnt, a little later, would make it "worth his while" to go back. This, if Sir John's statement in the House of Commons is to be trusted, the administration refused to pay.

And now some good priests made up their valises, and travelled out of the North-West, and all the way to Ottawa, to present the grievances of their people to the ministry. Archbishop Tache likewise showed himself at the capital on the same mission.

"For God's sake," these men said, "give earnest, careful, prompt attention to affairs in the North-West. The people have sore grievances, and they do not get the redress which is their due. If you would prevent mischief and misery, lose no time." And as in duty bound the politicians said: "The government will give the matter its most serious consideration."

M. Royal and the priests returned to the North-West down-spirited enough, and Mr. Macpherson sailed for England, while the half-breeds were making up their minds to obtain by force the rights which they had failed to obtain through peaceable means and persistent prayer.

CHAPTER XI.

The region known as Prince Albert was the chief seat of the disturbance. It has been already pointed out in these pages, that the connecting link between the Indian and the whiteman, is the half-breed. It is not to be wondered at then, that as soon as the Metis began to mutter vengeance against the authorities, the Indians began to hunt up their war paint. The writer is not seeking to put blame upon the Government, or upon the Department delegated especially to attend to Indian affairs, with respect to its management of the tribes. Any one who has studied the question at all, must know that there is nothing to be laid at the door of the Government in this regard.

A very clear statement of the whole question of Indian management, and of the assumption of the North-West Territories, may be found in Mr. Henry J. Morgan's Annual Register for 1878; while the same admirable work, gives from year to year, a capital *resume* of the condition of the tribes.

Some divines, recently in the North-west, have been discussing the Indian question in some of the religious newspapers of Toronto, but they have treated the question in the spirit of inexperienced spinsters. The Government has been most criminally remiss in their treatment of the half-breeds, but, let it be repeated, their Indian policy gives no ground for condemnation.

Yet when the half-breeds of Prince Albert, incited by Riel, began to collect fire-arms, and to drill in each others barns, the Indians began to sing and dance, and to brandish their tomahawks. Their way of living during late years has been altogether too slow, too dead-and-alive, too unlike the ways of their ancestors, when once at least in each year, every warrior returned to his lodge with scalp locks dangling at his belt. Les Gros-Ventres for the time, forgot their corporosity, and began to dance and howl, and declare that they would fight till all their blood was spilt with M. Riel, or his adjutant M. Dumont. The Blackfeet began to hold pow-wows, and tell their squaws that there would soon be good feasts. For many a day they had been casting covetous eyes upon the fat cattle of their white neighbours. Along too, came the feeble remnant of the once agile Salteaux, inquiring if it was to be war; and if so, would there be big feasts.

"O, big feasts, big feasts," was the reply. "Plenty fat cattle in the corals; and heaps of mange in the store." So the Salteaux were happy, and, somewhat in their old fashion, went vaulting homewards.

Tidings of fight, and feast, and turmoil reached the Crees, and they sallied out from the tents, while the large-eyed squaws sat silently reclining, marvelling what was to come of it all. High into the air the Nez Perce thrust his nostril; for he had got the scent of the battle from afar. And last, but not least, came the remnant of that tribe whose chief had shot Custer, in the Black Hills. The Sioux only required to be shown where the enemy lay; but in his enthusiasm he did not lose sight of the fat cattle grazing upon the prairies.

These, however, were only the first impulses of the tribes. Many of them now began to remember that the Government had shown them many kindnesses, given them tea and tobacco, and blankets; and provided them with implements to plough the lands, and oxen to draw the ploughs. And some of the chiefs came forward and said "You must not fight against the Great Mother. She loves the Indians. The red man is well treated here better than away south. Ask the Sioux who lived down there; they tell you maybe." Such advice served to set the Indians reflecting; but many hundreds of them preferred to hear Louis Riel's words, which were:—

"Indians have been badly treated. The Canadian Government has taken away their lands; the buffalo are nearly all gone, and Government sees the red men die of starvation without any concern. If you fight now you will make them dread you; and then they will be more liberal with you. Besides, during the war, you can have plenty of feasting among the fat cattle." A hellish war-whoop of approval always greeted such words.

At length the rising came. Gabriel Dumont, Riel's lieutenant, a courageous, skilful half-breed, possessed of a sound set of brains, had drilled several hundreds of the Indians and half-breeds. Armed with all sorts of guns, they collected, and stationed themselves near Duck Lake.

"My men," Dumont said, "You may not have to fight, for the officers may agree to the demand which I shall make of them on behalf of the Indians and the half-breed people. But if they refuse, and insist on passing, you know for what purpose you have taken arms into your hands. Let every shot be fired only after deliberate aim. Look to it that you fire low. After you have strewn the plain with their dead, they will go away with some respect for us. Then they will send out Commissioners to make terms with us. In the meantime the success of our attack, will bring hundreds of timid persons to our standard." This harangue was received with deafening cheers.

So the rebels posted themselves in the woods, and filled a sturdily built house near by, waiting for the approach of Major Crosier and his force. At last they were seen out upon the cold snow-covered prairie. A wild shout went up from the inmates of the house, and it was answered from tree to tree through all the wintry wood. In the exuberance of his delight, one Indian would yelp like a hungry wolf who sighted his prey; and another would hoot like an owl in the middle of the night. At last the police and civilians were close at hand. The meeting took place in a hollow. Beyond was the dim illimitable prairie, on either hand were clumps of naked, dismal poplar, and clusters of white oak. Snow was everywhere, and when a man moved the crunching of the crust could be heard far upon the chill air.

Signals were made for a parley, when some of the men from each side approached the line of demarcation. Joe McKay was the interpreter, and while he was speaking, an Indian, named Little Chief, grabbed at his revolver and tried to wrest it from him. A struggle ensued in which the Indian was worsted. Then raising his weapon McKay fired at the red skin, who dropped dead. This was the signal for battle. The voice of Dumont could be heard ringing through the hollow and over the hills. With perfect regularity his force spread out over a commanding bluff. Each man threw himself flat upon the ground, either shielding his body in the deep snow, or getting behind a tree or boulder. Major Crozier's force then drew their sleds across the trail, and the police threw themselves down behind it. Then came the words "Begin, my men," from the commander; —and immediately the crackle of rifles startled the hush of the wilderness. The police were lying down, yet they were not completely sheltered; but the civilians were standing.

"My God, I'm shot," said one, and he fell upon the snow, not moving again. Then, with a cry, another fell, and another. From the woods on every hand came the whistling shot, and the rushing slugs of the rebels. Every tree had behind it a rebel, with deadly aim. But the murderous bullets seemed to come out of the inanimate wilderness, for not no much as the hand that pulled the deadly trigger could be seen. The police had a mountain gun, which Major Crozier now ordered them to bring to bear on the rebels, but the policeman who loaded it was so confused that he put the lead in before the powder. In forty minutes the bloody fray was ended. Seven of the loyalists were dead in their blood upon the snow, two lay dying, eleven others were wounded and bleeding profusely, Then came the word to retire, when the Major's force drew off. From the bluff and out of all the woods now came diabolical yells and jeering shouts. The day belonged to the rebels.

When the police had moved away, the Indians and half-breeds came out from their ambush and began to hold rejoicings over the dead. They kicked the bodies, and then began to plunder them, getting, among other booty, two gold watches. Two of the fallen loyalists they observed still breathed, and these they shot through the head. So closely did they hold the muzzles of their murderous guns that the victims' faces were afterwards found discoloured with powder.

Then returning to camp, they secured seven prisoners whom they had captured, and, leading them to the battle-field, make them look at the stark bodies of the loyalists, at the same time heaping all manner of savage insult upon the dead.

A couple of days later the bodies of the victims were buried upon the plain, by the order of Riel. A little later the snow fell, and gave the poor fellows' grave a white, cold, coverlet.

When tidings of the battle, and of the defeat of our men, reached the east, the wildest excitement prevailed. At once the Minister of Militia began to take stock of his forces, and some regiments were ordered out. The volunteers needed no urging, but promptly offered their services for the front. Their loyalty was cheered to the echo, and thousands assembled at every railway station to see them depart and say "God speed."

CHAPTER XII.

While General Middleton, Colonel Otter, and others of our military officers, were hastening to the scene of tumult, tidings of the most startling kind were received from Frog Lake. Frog Lake is a small settlement, about forty miles north of Fort Pitt, and here a number of thrifty settlers had established themselves, tilling the soil. Latterly, however, some enterprising persons came there to erect a saw and grist mill, for much lumber fringes the lake, and a considerable quantity of grain is produced upon the prairie round about. There were only a few white settlers here, all the rest being half-breeds. Not far away lived detachments of various tribes of Indians, who frequently came into the little settlement, and smoked their pipes among the inhabitants. Here, as elsewhere, the most bitter feelings were entertained by the half-breeds and Indians against the Government, and chief of all against Governor Dewdney. Every one with white skin, and all those who in any way were in the service of the Government, soon came to be regarded as enemies to the common cause. Therefore, when night came down upon the settlement, Indians, smeared in hideous, raw, earthy-smelling paint, would creep about among dwellings, and peer, with eyes gleaming with hate, through the window-frames at the innocent and unsuspecting inmates. At last one chief, with a diabolical face, said,

"Brothers, we must be avenged upon every white man and woman here. We will shoot them like dogs. No harm can come to us; for the great man has said so." (Alluding to Riel.) "When they are all shot the Government will get a big fright, and give the Indians and half-breeds what they ask for." The answer to this harangue was the clanking of barbaric instruments of music, the brandishing of tomahawks, and the gleam of hunting-knives. Secretly the Indians went among the half-breeds squatting about, and revealed their plans; but some of these people shrank with fear from the proposal. Others, however, said,

"We shall join you. Let us with one blow wipe out the injustices done to us, and teach the Government that if they deny us our rights, we will fight for them; and murder those who are the agents of its will." So the plan was arranged, and it was not very long before it was carried out. And now runners were everywhere on the plains, telling that Dumont had a mighty army made up of most of the brave Indians of the prairies, and comprising all the dead shots among the half-breeds; that he had encountered heavy forces of police and armed civilians, and overthrown them without losing a single man. They likewise declared that he had hosts of prisoners, and that the whole of Canada was trembling with fear at the mention of the names of Riel and Dumont.

"Now is our time to strike," said the Indian with the fiendish face, and the wolf-like eyes.

Therefore, the 2nd day of April was fixed for the holding of the conference between the Indians and the white settlers. The malignant chief had settled the plan.

"When the white faces come to our lodge, they will expect no harm. Ugh! Then the red man will have his vengeance." So every Indian was instructed to have his rifle at hand in the lodge. The white folk wondered why the Indians had arranged for a conference.

"We can do nothing to help their case," they said, "we ourselves find it difficult enough to get the ear of Government. It will only waste time to go." Many of them, therefore, remained at home, occupying themselves with their various duties, while the rest, merely for the sake of agreeableness, and of shewing the Indians that they were interested in their affairs, proceeded to the place appointed for the pow-wow.

"We hope to smoke our pipes before our white brothers go away from us," was what the treacherous chief, with wolfish eyes, had said, in order to put the settlers off their guard.

The morning of the 2nd opened gloomily, as if it could not look cheerily down upon the bloody events planned in this distant wilderness. Low, indigo clouds looked down over the hills, but there was not a stir in all the air. Nor was any living thing to be seen stirring, save that troops of blue-jays went scolding from tree to tree before the settlers as they proceeded to the conference, and they perceived a few half-famished, yellow, and black and yellow dogs, with small heads and long scraggy hair, sculking about the fields and among the wigwams of the Indians in search for food.

The lodge where the parley was to be held stood in a hollow. Behind was a tall bluff, crowned with timber; round about it green poplar, white oak, and some firs, while in front rolled by a swift stream, which had just burst its winter fetters. Unsuspecting aught of harm, two priests of the settlement, Oblat Fathers, named Fafard and La Marchand, were the first at the spot.

"What a gloomy day," Pere Fafard said, "and this lodge set here in this desolate spot seems to make it more gloomy still. What, I wonder, is the nature of the business?" Then they knocked, and the voice of the chief was heard to say,

"Entrez." Opening the door, the two good priests walked in, and turned to look for seats. Ah! what was the sight presented to them! Eyes like those of wild beasts, aflame with hate and ferocity, gleamed at them from the gloom of the back portion of the room. The priests were amazed. They knew not what all this meant. Then a wild shriek was given, and the chief cried, "Enemies to the red man, you have come to your doom." Then raising his rifle, he fired at Father Marchand. The levelling of his rifle was the general signal. A dozen other muzzles were pointed, and in a far briefer space of time than it takes to relate it, the two priests lay weltering in their blood, pierced each by half a dozen bullets.

"Clear away these corpses," shouted the chief, "and be ready for the next." There was soon another knock at the door, and the same wolfish voice replied as before, saying,

"Entrez." This time a full, manly-looking young fellow, named Charles Gowan, opened the door and entered. Always on the alert for Indian treachery, he had his suspicion now, before entering he suspected strongly that all was not right. He had only reached the settlement that morning, and had he returned sooner he would have counselled the settlers to pay no heed to the invitation. He was assured that several had already gone up to the pow-wow, so being brave and unselfish, he said,

"If there is any danger afoot, and my friends are at the meeting-lodge, that is the place for me, not here." He had no sooner entered than his worst convictions were realized. With one quick glance he saw the bloodpools, the wolfish eyes, the rows of ready rifles.

"Hell hounds!" he cried, "what bloody work have you on hand? What means this?" pointing to the floor.

"It means," replied the chief, "that some of your pale-face brethren have been losing their heart's blood there. It also means that the same fate awaits you." Resolved to sell his life as dearly as lay in his power, he sprang forward with a Colt's revolver, and discharged it twice. One Indian fell, and another set up a cry like the bellowing of a bull. But poor Gowan did not fire a third shot. A tall savage approached him from behind, and striking him upon the head with his rifle-stock felled him to the earth. Then the savages fired five or six shots into him as he lay upon the floor. The body was dragged away and the blood-thirsty fiends sat waiting for the approach of another victim. Half an hour passed, and no other rap came upon the door. An hour went, and still no sound of foot-fall. All this while the savages sat mute as stones, each holding his murderous rifle in readiness for instant use.

"Ugh!" grunted the chief, "no more coming. We go down and shoot em at em houses." Then the fiend divided his warriors into four companies, each one of which was assigned a couple of murders. One party proceeded toward the house of Mr. Gowanlock, of the firm of Gowanlock & Laurie, who had a large saw and grist mill in course of erection; creeping stealthily along, and concealing their approach by walking among the trees they were within forty yards of the house without being perceived. Then Mrs. Gowanlock, a young woman, recently married, walked out of the house, and gathering some kindling-wood in her apron, returned again. When the Indians saw her, they threw themselves upon their faces, and so escaped observation. Little did the inmates know the deadly danger that so closely menaced them. They went on talking cheerfully, dreaming of no harm. Gowanlock, as I have said, had been recently married, and himself and his young wife were buoyant with hope, for the future had already begun to promise them much. Mr. Gowanlock had gathered the wood with which to make biscuits; and W. C. Gilchrist, and Williscroft, two fine young men, both in Mr. Gowanlock's employ, were chatting with him on general matters. No one happened to be looking out of the window after Mrs. Gowanlock came in; but about half a minute afterwards some shadow flitted by the window, and immediately afterwards six or seven painted Indians, with rifles cocked, and uttering diabolical yells, burst into the house. The chief was with this party; and aiming his rifle, shot poor Gowanlock dead, another aimed at Gilchrist, but Mrs. Gowanlock heroically seized the savage's arms from behind, and prevented him for a moment or two; but the vile murderer shook her off, and falling back a pace or two, fired at her, killing her instantly. Three had now fallen, and as the poor young wife fell crying, "my God!" Croft fell pierced by two or three bullets. Lest the work might not have been sufficiently done, the murderers fired once more at the fallen victims, and then came away from the house.

One of the most deserving of the settlers, but at the same time one of the most bitterly hated, was Dunn, the Indian agent. He was a half breed, and had for a wife a very pretty Cree woman. For some days past, it is said, that she had been aware that the massacre had been planned; but uttered no word of warning. Stealthily the blood-thirsty band approached the dwelling of Dunn, for they knew him to be a brave man, who would sell his life very dearly. They were aware that in the Minnesota massacre which happened some years ago, that he had fought as if his life were charmed, and escaped with a few trifling wounds. The doomed man was alone on this terrible day, his wife having taken her blanket at an early hour and gone abroad to "talk" with some Cree maidens. Poor Dunn was busy in the little yard behind his house, putting handles in some of his farming implements, and did not perceive the approach of the murderers at all. There were five Indians in the party, and they crept up to within a dozen paces of where the unsuspecting man was at his work. Then, while he whistled a merry tune, they silently raised their rifles and took aim. The unfortunate man fell, pierced with all their bullets and made no stir.

Another detachment of the bloodhounds directed their steps towards the residence of Barnez Fremoine, the Belgian rancher. He was a tall, magnificently-built man, and when the savages got in sight of his house they perceived that he was engaged oiling the axle of his waggon.

Aided by the shelter of an outhouse, they approached within twenty yards of this victim; raised their arms and arrows and fired. He fell likewise without uttering a cry, and made no stir. When found afterwards there were two bullet holes in his head, and an arrow lay lodged in his breast. [Footnote: This fact I get from correspondence to the Ottawa *Free Press*, a newspaper which, under the great journalistic enterprise of Mr. J. T. Hawke, has kept the people at the Capital well informed from day to day on affairs at the scene of tumult.] Two other persons were surprised in the same way, and shot down like dogs, making a total of eleven slaughtered.

The first official confirmation of the dreadful tragedy was given in a despatch, sent from Fort Pitt to Sir John Macdonald, by police inspector Dickens, a son of the immortal novelist.

CHAPTER XIII.

Perhaps, of all the acts of bravery recorded during this late Rebellion, not one stands out more prominently than that of Inspector Dickens, in resisting, with his little force, a large band of blood-thirsty Crees, till he would, with advantage and honour, retire from his ground. Fort Pitt stands in the centre of the Cree country, and was the scene of the treaty between the Government and the Crees, Chippewayans, Assinniboines and the Chippewas. There was great difficulty at the time in concluding the terms of the treaty. Big Bear, who reigns supreme in the district, and who was spokesman at the treaty, maintained that hanging ought to be abolished, and the buffalo protected. On the whole, he accepted the conditions of the treaty, but, as his people were not present, he would not sign it, although he did sign it in the following year. Big Bear is a noisy, meddlesome savage, who is never in his glory save when he is the centre of some disturbance. He has always shown much delight in talking about war; and he would go without his meals to listen to a good story about fighting. He has the habit to, when the reciter of the story has finished, of trying to discount what he has heard, and to make his auditors believe that some exploits of his own have been far more thrilling. When everything is peaceable, even when there are plenty of buffalo and peltry to be had, this savage is not satisfied; but still goes around asking if there is any news about trouble being about to take place anywhere. If he is told:

"No, everything is quiet; the Indians are all satisfied, because they are doing well." Big Bear will reply, while knowingly closing one eye:

"Me know better than that. There will soon be bloody work. Government break em treaty with Injuns. Lots of Injuns now ready to go out and scalp servants of the Government and white men." When, therefore, tidings reached the land of the Stoney Indians that the half-breeds, with Louis Riel at their head, had broken into revolt, Big Bear pulled off his feathered cap and threw it several times into the air. He went to his wives, a goodly number of which he is in the habit of keeping, and informed them that he would soon bring them home some scalps. He was so elated, that he ordered several of the young men to go and fetch him several white dogs to make a feast. So a large fire was built upon the prairie, a short distance from the chief's lodge, and the huge festival pot was suspended from a crane over the roaring flames. First, about fifteen gallons of water were put into this pot; then Big Bear's wives, some of whom were old and wrinkled, and others of which were lithe as fawns, plump and bright-eyed, busied themselves gathering herbs. Some digged deep into the marsh for roots of the "dog-bane," others searched among the knotted roots for the little nut-like tuber that clings to the root of the flag, while others brought to the pot wild parsnips, and the dried stalks of the prairie pusley. A coy little maiden, whom many a hunter had wooed but failed to win, had in her sweet little brown hands a tangle of winter-green, and maiden-hair. Then came striding along the young hunters, with the dogs. Each dog selected for the feast was white as the driven snow. If a black hair, or a blue hair, or a brown hair, was discovered anywhere upon his body he was taken away; but if he were *sans reproche* he was put, just as he was, head, and hide, and paws, and tail on—his throat simply having been cut—into the pot, Six dogs were thrown in, and the roots and stalks of the prairie plants, together with salt, and bunches of the wild pepper-plant, and of swamp mustard were thrown in for seasoning. Through the reserves round about for many miles swarth heralds proclaimed that the great Chief Big Bear was giving a White Dog feast to his braves before summoning them to follow him upon the war-path. The feast was, in Indian experience, a magnificent one, and before the young men departed they swore to Big Bear that they returned only for their war-paint and arms, and that before the set of the next sun they would be back at his side.

True to their word the Indians came, hideous in their yellow paint. If you stood to leeward of them upon the plain a mile away you could clearly get the raw, earthy smell of the ochre upon their hands and faces. Some had black bars streaked across their cheeks, and hideous crimson circles about their eyes. Some, likewise, had stars in pipe-clay painted upon the forehead.

Now the immediate object of the warlike enthusiasm of all these young men was the capture of Fort Pitt, an undertaking which they hardly considered worth shouldering their rifles for. But when it came to the actual taking it was a somewhat different matter. There were twenty-one policemen in the Fort and they had at their head an intrepid chief, Mr. Inspector Dickens, already referred to in this chapter. It was useless to fire bullets at the solid stockades; massacre was out of the question, for keen eyes peered ever from the Fort. Big Bear now had grown very ambitious.

"Fort Pitt hardly worth bothering about," he said to his braves. "Plenty of big fighting everywhere. We'll go with Monsieur Riel. But we must have guns; good guns; and plenty of powder and shot and ball. So taking a number of his braves he approached the Fort and began to bellow that he wanted to have a talk. Inspector Dickens appeared, calling out,

"Well, what does Big Bear want?"

"We want guns, and powder, and shot, and ball."

"Pray, what does Big Bear want with them?"

"His young men are suffering of hunger, and they want to go shoot some elk and bear."

"Big Bear is talking with a crooked tongue. He must not have any rifles, or powder or shot, or ball. I advise him to return peaceably to his reserve; and if there is anything that the Government can do for himself, or his people, I am sure they will do it. He will only make matters worse by creating a disturbance."

"Ugh! The great police chief also talks with a crooked tongue; and if he does not give what the Indians ask for, they will burn down the fort, and murder himself and his followers, not sparing either the women or the children."

"If this be your intention, you shall not find us unprepared." Just at this moment two mounted police, who had been out upon the plains as scouts, came in sight, at once Inspector Dickens perceived that the savages meant mischief. A number of rifles were raised at the unsuspecting policemen, then several shots were heard. Constable Cowan fell from his horse dead, pierced by several bullets; Constable Lousby was hit by a couple of bullets, but got into the fort before the savages could prevail.

"Now, my men," shouted Inspector Dickens, "show these insolent savages that you can defy them." At once a raking fire was poured into the rebels. Four of the rebels fell dead, and some scores of others were wounded. The conduct of some of the savages who received slight wounds was exceedingly ludicrous. One who had been shot, *in running away*, began to yell in the most pitiable way; and he ran about the plain kicking up his heels and grabbing at the wounded spot, which, it is to be inferred, must have been stinging him very badly. I must not omit to speak that before the *recontre*, chief factor MacLean, who had always been held in high regard among the Indians, went out of the fort to have a parley with Big Bear. Arriving at the door of the chief's lodge, he knocked. Big Bear admitted him with the greatest pleasure, and after he had done so, said:

"Guess me keep you, since me's get you." So the chief factor found himself a prisoner. Then Big Bear informed his captive that if he would write a letter to the rest of the civilians in the fort, asking them to withdraw, and enter into the Indian lodge, he would treat them civilly; but that if they refused, he would set fire to the fort, and they would perish in the flames. This MacLean consented to do, and in a little while there went out from the fort to the Indian prison, Mr. MacLean's family, consisting of eight, James Simpson, Stanley Simpson, W. B. Cameron, one Dufresne, Rev. C. Quinn, and his wife, and Mr. and Mrs. Mann, with their three children. Since that date, these people have been prisoners in Big Bear's camp, and every now and again the tidings come that they are receiving barbarous, and even brutal, treatment. After Big Bear had got possession of all these, he said to his chief young men:

"'Spose we take em in, too, Mounted Police. No harm Get their guns. Keep them here for a spell, and then let 'em go." When he coolly presented himself before the stockades and proposed to Inspector Dickens to come right over to his lodges, assuring him that he would not allow the hair of one of his men's heads to be harmed, Inspector Dickens laughed:

"You are a very presumptuous savage." After the fight which I have described, Inspector Dickens, studying the situation, regarded it in this light:

"The civilians have gone to the Indians, so there is now no object to be attained by keeping my force here. In the battle with the savages I was successful. Therefore, may retreat with honour." Fitting up a York boat, he had it provisioned for the journey, and then destroying everything in the shape of supplies, arms and ammunition Which he could not take away, they started down the river, and after a tedious journey arrived at Battleford, worn with anxious watching, exposure and fatigue, but otherwise safe and well, save for the wounded constable. The brave Inspector was received at Battleford with ringing acclamations. Here, in a little, he was appointed to the command of the Police, superseding Lt.-Colonel Morris. Altogether there is not in the whole campaign an instance in which good judgment and bravery stand out so prominently as in this record of the conduct of the son of our great English novelist.

CHAPTER XIV.

No accident in the whole history of the present rebellion so ill bears to be written about as does this of the sacking of Battleford. This is a town of considerable importance, and it has a strongly-built fort, garrisoned by mounted police. It stands close to a large Cree reserve, and the prairie around it being very fertile, the population latterly had been growing rapidly. When first the disturbance broke out, it was feared that there would be trouble with the Stoney Crees in this region; for Poundmaker, a great brawling Indian chief, is always ready, like his boastful brother, Big Bear, to join in any revolt against authority. Poundmaker, for many a year, has done little save to smoke, drink tea among the squaws, and tell lies, as long as the Saskatchewan river, about all the battles he fought when he was a young man, and how terrible was his name over all the plains. Poundmaker has always been successful as a boaster, and there is hardly a squaw on the whole reserve who does not think him to be one of the most illustrious and mighty men alive. Therefore he has never sued in vain for the hand of a pretty maiden without success; and he has now no fewer than a score of wives, whom he is not able to support, and who are therefore compelled to go on their bare brown feet among the marshes in the summer, killing frogs and muskrats. The lazy rascal never works, but sits at home drinking strong tea, smoking and telling lies, while his wives, young ones and old ones, and his brawling papooses go abroad looking for something to eat.

Now besides Poundmaker, there were among those Stoney Crees two other mischief-loving half-and-half Chiefs. One delighted in the name of Lucky Man, and the other of Little Pine. These two vagabonds leagued themselves with Poundmaker, when the first tidings of the the outbreak reached them, and painting their faces, went abroad among the young men, inciting them to revolt. They reminded them, that if they arose they would have plenty of big feasts, for the prairie was full of the white men's cattle. And Little Pine glanced with snaky eyes toward the town of Battleford.

"May be by-em-by, get fine things out of stores. Go in and frighten away 'em people, then take heaps o' nice things; get squaws, may be, to help 'em to carry 'em away." This was just the sort of incentive that the young men wanted; and the Indian girls screamed with delight at the prospect of red shawls, and heaps of ribbons, and boxes of brass rings, and pretty red and white stockings, and boots with buttons on them.

Presently Big Bear, and Little Pine, and Lucky Man began to get their forces in motion. Armed with bows and arrows, spears, and tomahawks, shot-guns and flint-muskets, and followed by gew-gaw-loving girls, squalling pappooses, and half starved yellow dogs, the Crees, with the three beauties just mentioned at their head, marched toward the town. The people, apprised of the intended attack, had fled to the police barracks; so that when the savages entered the town, the streets were deserted. Then commenced the work of pillage. According to a correspondent of the *Montreal Star*, "house after house was visited in quick succession, the squaws loudly acclaiming and shouting as the bucks smashed in the doors with axes. Firearms were the first things sought for by the braves, while the females ransacked each dwelling from top to bottom, in search of such articles as delighted the feminine eye, Soon the hitherto quiet and peaceful town of Battleford was transformed into a veritable place of destruction. Torn carpets, chairs, bedsteads and empty trunks were thrown into the streets, which were thronged by at least 500 Indians, who, made hideous with war paint, shouted and discharged their rifles simultaneously, creating a perfect pandemonium. When the pillagers had accomplished their work, they commenced the attack on the barracks, but were repulsed with a trifling loss. Some young bucks got rolls of carpet, which they extended along the street, and then mounting their ponies rode up and down over the aesthetic patterns. The squaws got fineries enough to deck themselves in for the next year; and the amount of brass rings that they carried away was enough to make glad the heart of all Indian-dom. After having surfeited themselves with destruction, they returned, each one laden to his and her utmost capacity with booty. Several places were gutted and demolished; in other cases property was destroyed, and some establishments were set on fire."

All this while Major Morris and his police, and nearly two hundred able bodied men, with 200 rifles and plenty of ammunition were cooped up in the Fort, peeping out at the squaws pillaging the town. It seems a little illogical that we should call out our young men from Halifax, from Quebec, from Montreal, from Kingston, from Ottawa, and from the other cities that put forces into the field, to go out into the far wilderness to protect property, when able-bodied men with arms in their hands stood by and watched unmoved a body of savages and squaws pillage their town, and give their property to the flames. It was to relieve this town that Colonel Otter made the brilliant march, upon which writers and orators have not been able to bestow enough of eulogy.

CHAPTER XV.

After the defeat of the police and civilians at Duck Lake, Riel and Dumont felt thoroughly confident of being able to deal with the forces which they were apprised the Canadian Government would send into the field against them. They held many long consultations together, and in every case it was Dumont who laid down the details of the military campaign. "These Canadian soldiers," he would say, "can not fight us here. We will entrench ourselves in positions against which they may fire cannon or gatling guns in vain. They are not used to bush-fighting, and will all the time expose themselves to our bullets. Besides, distances here are deceptive; and in their confusion they will make the wildest sort of shooting." It was decided that the rebel forces should make their main stand at an advantageous position, which Dumont had accidentally observed one day when he was out elk-stalking three years ago. This place, he assured his chief seemed to be intended by nature for a post of defence. It lay a short distance from Batoche's Crossing.

"But my idea is to engage them several times with portions of my force; gradually to fall back, and then fight at my final ground the battle which shall decide who is master in these territories, the half-breeds or the Canadian volunteers."

All this while General Middleton, with his brave fellows, had been making one of the most laborious marches recorded in modern wars. Perhaps the worst portion of the march was around the dismal reaches of Lake Superior. I take an extract from correspondence to the Toronto *Mail*. "But the most severe trial was last night's, in a march from Red Rock to Nepigon, a distance of only seven miles across the ice, yet it took nearly five hours to do it. After leaving the cars the battalion paraded in line. A couple of camp fires served to make the darkness visible. All the men were anxious to start, and when the word was given to march, it was greeted with cheers. It was impossible to march in fours, therefore an order was given for left turn, quick march. We turned, obedient to the order, but the march was anything but quick. Then into the solemn darkness of the pines and hemlock the column slowly moved. Each side being snow four feet deep, it was almost impossible to keep the track, and a misstep buried the unfortunate individual up to his neck. Then it began raining, and for three mortal hours there was a continuous down pour. The lake was reached at last, to the extreme pleasure of the corps. The wildness of the afternoon and the rain turned the snow into slush, at every step the men sank half a foot. All attempts to preserve distance were soon abandoned by the men, who clasped hands to prevent falling. The officers struggled on, arms linked, for the same purpose. Now and then men would drop in the ranks, the fact only being discovered by those in the rear stumbling over them. Some actually fell asleep as they marched. One brave fellow had plodded on without a murmur for three days. He had been suffering, but through the fear of being left behind in the hospital refrained from making his case known. He tramped half-way across last night's march reeling like a drunken man, but nature gave out at last, and with a groan he fell on the snow. There he lay, the pitiless rain beating on a boyish upturned face, until a passing sleigh stopped behind him. The driver, flashing his lantern in the upturned face, said he was dead. 'Not yet, old man,' was the reply of the youth, as he opened his eyes. 'I'm not even a candidate for the hospital yet.'"

The following description of the Great Salt Plains, as given by a *Globe* correspondent, is also worth reproducing: "The Great Salt Plains open out like broad, dreary marsh or arm of the sea, from which the tide has gone out. For about thirty-five miles the trail stretches in a north-westerly course across this dismal expanse, and away to the south-west, as far as the eye can reach, nothing save marsh grass, flags, bullrushes, and occasionally clumps of marsh willows can be seen. North-east of the trail scattering bluffs of stunted grey willows cluster along the horizon, and at one point along the trail, about midway of the plain, is found a small, solitary clump of stoneberry bushes, not more than thirty yards long, five or six feet in width, and only three or four feet high." The objective point of Major-General Middleton's march was Batoche's Crossing, where Riel had several large pits sunk, and fortifications thrown up, for a grand and final encounter with our troops. The line of march lay sometimes along the Saskatchewan's banks, but more frequently through the open prairie. The position of the rebels prior to the battle was this: Dumont, with 250 half-breeds and Indians, had been retreating slowly before General Middleton's right column on the east bank of the river, their scouts keeping them informed of the General's movements. Dumont appears to have thought of waiting for the troops to attack him on Thursday night; at least that is the belief of the scouts, who saw some of his mounted men signalling to him all afternoon on Thursday. However that may be, he lay waiting for our men at the edge of a big *coulee* near Fish Creek, early on Friday morning, his forces being snugly stowed away behind boulders, or concealed in the dense everglades of hazel, birch, and poplar. From day to day, almost from hour to hour, this veteran buffalo hunter had learned every tidings of the General's troops that keen observation made from clumps of bush along the prairie could give him. So when he learnt that the General himself, with his officers, were near at hand, his eyes fairly gleamed with enthusiasm.

"My men," he said, as he went from covert to covert, from bluff to bluff, "you know the work that lies before you; I need not repeat it to you. Do not expose yourself, and do not fire unless you have a tolerable target." Then he arranged a system of signals, chiefly low whistles and calls, by which the men would be able to know when to advance, retire, lie close, make a dash, or move from one part of the ground to another.

"They will at first fall into an ambush," he said, "then, my men, be nimble. In the panic there will be a rich harvest for you. Bring down the General if you can. Wherever an officer is in range, let him have a taste of your lead in preference to the privates." Then he lay close and watched, and listened, many times putting his ear to the ground. At last he gave an exclamation. It was in a whisper; but the silent rebels who lay there, mute as the husht trees around them, could well hear the words, "they come!"

Let me now briefly describe the position which the rebel had chosen for himself. About five miles from McIntosh's stand two bluffs, about five hundred yards apart, thickly wooded on the top. Between these bluffs is a level open prairie that extends backward about a thousand yards, across which there runs a deep ravine, thickly timbered at the bottom.

Now, on the morning of Friday, the twenty-fourth of April, General Middleton, who was still on the march to Batoche's, was riding with his staff, well in front. With him was Major Boulton's Horse, who acted as scouts. As they were passing the two bluffs named, suddenly the crack of musketry rang out upon the prairie. Major Boulton now perceived that he had fallen into an ambush. At the same time that deadly balls and buck-shot came whistling and cutting spitefully through the air, there arose from both bluffs the most diabolical yelling. For miles over the silent prairies could these murderous yells be heard. Nor were the rebel balls fired without effect. Captain Gardner fell bleeding upon the ground, and several of the men had also fallen.

General Middleton, who had been some little distance in the rear was speedily apprised of the surprise, and dashing on toward the rebels' hold he met Boulton's Horse retiring for reinforcements. Then "A" Battery, the 90th regiment, and "C" Company, Toronto, with enthusiastic cheering, began to cry out: "Show us the rebels!"

In a little while the firing became general, and our men struck out extending their formation as they neared the edge of the *coulee*, from which puffs of smoke were already curling up. Twenty of Dumont's men, with Winchesters, fired over a natural shelf or parapet protected by big boulders. The column was divided into two wings, the left consisting of "B" and "F" Companies of the 90th, with Boulton's mounted corps, and the right of the rest of the 90th, "A" Battery, and "C" School of Infantry. The left wing, "F" company leading, came under fire first. As the men were passing by him; Gen. Middleton shouted out:

"Men of the 90th, don't bend your heads; you will soon be there; go in, and I know you'll do your duty."

The men were bending down, partly to avoid the shots and partly because they were running over the uneven, scrubby ground. Colour-Sergeant Mitchell, of "F" company (one of the famous Wimbledon Mitchells), displayed great coolness, and afterwards did good execution with a rifle when the troops had entered the bush. "A," "C," and "D" Companies of the 90th, with "A" Battery and the School of Infantry, were on the right, the whole force forming a huge half-moon around the mouth of the *coulee*. The brush was densely thick, and as rain was falling, the smoke hung in clouds a few feet off the muzzles of the rifles.

Here the 90th lost heavily. Ferguson was the first to fall. The bandsmen came up and carried off the injured to the rear, where Dr. Whiteford and other surgeons had extemporized a small camp, the men being laid some on camp-stretchers and some on rude beds of branches and blankets. "E" company of the 90th, under Capt. Whitla, guarded the wounded and the ammunition. General Middleton appeared to be highly pleased with the bearing of the 90th as they pushed on, and repeatedly expressed his admiration. He seemed to think, however, that the men exposed themselves unnecessarily. When they got near the *coulee* in skirmishing order, they fired while lying prostrate, but some of them either through nervousness or a desire to get nearer the unseen enemy, kept rising to their feet, and the moment they did so Dumont's men dropped them with bullets or buckshot. The rebels, on the other hand, kept low. They loaded, most of them having powder and shot bags below the edge of the ravine or behind the thicket, and then popped up for an instant and fired. They had not time to take aim except at the outset, when the troops were advancing.

Meanwhile the right wing had gone into action also. Two guns of "A" Battery, under Capt. Peters, dashed up at 10:40 o'clock, and at once opened on the *coulee*. A couple of old barns far back to the right were knocked into splinters at the outset, it being supposed that rebels were concealed there; and three haystacks were bowled over and subsequently set on fire by the shells or fuses. Attention was then centred on the ravine. At first, however, the battery's fire had no effect, as from the elevation on which the guns stood, the shot went whizzing over it. Dumont had sent thirty men to a small bluff, covered with boulder and scrub, within 450 yards of the battery, and these opened a sharp fire. The battery could not fire into this bluff without running the risk of killing some of the 90th, who had worked their way up towards the right of it. Several men of "A" were struck here. The rebels saw that their sharpshooters were causing confusion in this quarter, and about twenty of them ran clear from the back of the ravine past the fire of "C" and "D" companies to the bluff, and joined their comrades in a rattling fusillade on "A." Fortunately, only a few of them, had Winchesters. "A" moved forward a little, and soon got the measure of the ravine. The shrapnel screeched in the air, and burst right in among the brush and boulders, smashing the scraggy trees, and tearing up the moss that covered the ground in patches. The rebels at once saw that the game was up in this quarter, though they kept up a bold front and seldom stopped firing except when they were dodging back into new cover. In doing this they rarely exposed themselves, either creeping on all fours or else running a few yards in the shelter of the thicket and then throwing themselves flat on the ground again, bobbing up only when they raised their heads and elbows to fire.

The shrapnel was too much for them, and they began to bolt towards the other side of the ravine, where our left wing was peppering them. This move was the first symptom of weakness they had exhibited, and Gen. Middleton at once took advantage of it and ordered the whole force to close in upon them, his object apparently being to surround them. The rebel commander, however, was not to be caught in that way. Instead of bunching all his forces on the left away from the fire of the artillery, he sent only a portion of it there to keep our men busy while the rest filled off to the north, retiring slowly as our two wings closed on them. Dumont was evidently on the look-out for the appearance of Col. Montizambert's force from the other side of the river.

The general advance began at 11.45 a.m., Major Buchan of the 90th leading the right wing, and Major Boswell of the same corps the left. When the rebels saw this a number of them rushed forward on the left of the ravine, and the fighting for a time was carried on at close quarters, the enemy not being over sixty yards away. An old log hut and a number of barricades, formed by placing old trees and brushwood between the boulders, enabled them to make it exceedingly warm for our men for a time. At this point several of the 90th were wounded, and General Middleton himself had a narrow escape, a bullet going through his fur hat. Captains Wise and Doucet, of Montreal, the General's Aide-de-camps, were wounded about this time. "C" infantry behaved remarkably well all through, and bore the brunt of the general advance for some time, the buckshot from the rebels doing much damage. The rebel front was soon driven back, but neither here nor at any other time could the rebels' loss be ascertained. The Indians among them, who were armed with guns, appeared to devote themselves mainly to shooting the horses. A good many Indians were hit, and every time one of them was struck the others near him raised a loud shout, as if cheering. The troops pressed on gallantly, and the rebel fire slackened, and after a time died away, though now and then their front riflemen made a splurge, while the others made their way back. Captain Forrest, of the 90th, headed the advance at this point, Lieutenant Hugh J. Macdonald (son of Sir John Macdonald), of this company, who had done excellent service all day, kept well up with Forrest, the two being ahead of their men, and coming in for a fair share of attention from the retreating rebels. Macdonald was first reported as killed and then as wounded, but he was not injured, though struck on the shoulder by spent buckshot. Forrest's hat was shot off. At 12.50 the rebels were far out of range, going towards Batoche's, and the Battle of Fish Creek was practically over. [Footnote: I am chiefly indebted to the Toronto *Mail* for the foregoing account of the battle.]

During the battle, many instances of the greatest bravery are recorded. Private Ainsworth, of the 90th, was seen to leap upon the shoulders of a savage, who, in company with another, had endeavoured to cross the flat land and get shelter, wresting his gun and felling him to the earth with the butt of it, then securing the rifle firing at and killing the other Indian. While doing this, he was exposed to the fire of a score of guns, getting riddled with buck-shot and being struck with bullets. But the greatest daring and bravery were exhibited by Watson, of the Toronto School of Infantry. Finding it impossible to dislodge the enemy, he rushed headlong for the ambuscaded half-breeds, followed by a score of his comrades whom it was impossible to control. The war-cries of the Indians, the huzzas of the troops, and the rattle of musketry fairly echoed for miles, as evidenced by the statements of the west side contingent upon arriving on the scene. Watson paid the penalty of his daring by death, while the narrow escape of many others were remarkable. The utmost bravery all the while was displayed by our troops. When a man fell his comrade would pause for a moment, and say:

"I hope you are not badly hurt," and then again look out for the enemy. Some of the men who received only slight wounds were anxious to remain in the fight, but their officers insisted that they should be taken to the rear, and attended to by the surgeons. Upon couches made of boughs, and covered with blankets, the brave young fellows were placed; and many of them submitted to probings and painful management of wounds without making a murmur. They seemed not to be concerned for themselves, but went on all the while enquiring as to how it was "going with the boys."

General Middleton, himself a veteran soldier, expressed as I have already stated, his admiration for the bravery of all the men who were engaged. There was no bolting, even in the face of heavy fire; no shrinking, although *one man in every eight* had been struck by the enemy's shot or bullets. Major Boulton had many narrow escapes, while he was standing for a moment, a hail of buckshot came whistling by his ear, burying itself into his horse, which was killed instantly. The Scouts, known as Boulton's Horse, under this brave officer, bore very gallantly their portion of the battle's brunt. Half-breads and Indians had orders from their leaders to shoot down horses as well as men; and Dumont frequently said, that the mounted men were the only ones of the force of the enemy for which he cared anything. Several of the horses were shot, and many of the men were riddled with buck-shot, but they bravely stood their ground. In the night, when the weary were sleeping after the hard day's work, dusky forms could be seen by the light of the moon, creeping stealthily towards where slept the gallant Scouts. The Guard heard a crackle, and turning, perceived three pairs of eyes gleaming with ferocity in the shadow of a clump of poplars.

"Qui vive?" he cried, and raised his rifle; but before he could take aim, three shots rang out through the still night, and he fell dead, pierced by as many bullets. There was a general alarm through the camp, but no eye could detect the form of a Rebel. They were safe among the shadows in the ravine. In the few moments of silent horror that ensued after the commission of the murder, three diabolical yells sounded from the ravine, and far over the moon-lit prairies. Then divers voices were heard in the bluffs, and down in the gorge. These came from Dumont's men, who jeered, and cried that they hoped the soldiers enjoyed the pastime of watching their dead.

On the following day, the bodies of the brave young fellows who had fallen, after being decently, and decorously disposed in death, were brought to the graves hollowed out in this far-away wilderness by the hands of old comrades. It was a very sad spectacle indeed. The death of brave soldiers is always mournful to contemplate; but war is the *trade* of regulars, and they expect death, and burials in distant sod. But war is not the trade of our volunteer soldiers. They are mere young fellows, of various pursuits of life, and death and burial away from home lose nothing of their sorrowful surroundings, because the taking off has been at the hands of rebel murderers. General Middleton conducted the ceremonies; and here upon the wide, husht prairie, which will soon deck the graves with flowers, they were laid away. The brave young fellows who faced the Rebels' shot and ball without failing, faltered now, and many of them wept copious tears.

On the following day, General Middleton began to make ready for his march toward Batoche's, where the Rebels' stronghold is located. Meanwhile the following sick and wounded have been left at the hospital at dark's Crossing, under the care of Dr. Orton: Captain Clark; Privates Hislop, Harris, Stovel, Matthews, Code Jarvis, Canniff, Lethbridge, Kemp, Bruce; Captain Gardner; Privates Perrin, King, Dunn, McDonald,

Cummings, Jones, R. Jones, Wilson, Morrison, Woodman, Imrie, Asseline, Lailor; Sergeant Mawhinney, Private Wainwright.

The following is a list of the killed and wounded from the outbreak of the Rebellion to the close of Colonel Otter's engagement with Pound maker, Big Bear and other Indian bands:—

Killed at Prince Albert:—

Constable T. G. Gibson; Constable G. P. Arnold; Constable Garrett; Capt. John Morton; W. Napier; C. Page; James Blakey; J. Napier Elliott; Robert Middleton; D. Mackenzie; D. McPhail; Charles Newitt; Joseph Anderson; Alexander Fisher.

Wounded at Prince Albert:—

Capt. Moore; A. MacNab; Alex. Stewart; Inspector J. Howe; Corporal Gilchrist; S. F. Gordon; A. W. Smith; J. J. Moore; A. Miller.

Killed at Frog Lake:—

T. T. Quinn, Indian Agent at Frog Lake; Father Fafard; Father Marchand; John Delaney, Farm Inspector; J. A. Gowanlock; Mrs. Gowanlock; Charles Gouin; William Gilchrist; Two Lay Brothers; John Williscraft; James K. Simpson, and two Hudson Bay men made prisoners, and probably murdered by Frog Lake Indians.

Killed at Fort Pitt:—

Constable Cowan, N. W. M. P.

Wounded at Fort Pitt:—

Constable Lonsley, N. W. M. P

Killed at Fish Creek:—

Lieut. Swinford, 90th; Private Hutchinson, No. 1 Company, 90th; Private Ferguson, No. 1 Company, 90th; Private Ennis, No. 4 Company, 90th; Gunner Demanolly, "A" Battery; Arthur Watson, School of Infantry; D'Arcy Baker, Mounted Infantry; Gunner Cook, "A" Battery; Wheeler, 90th; Ainsworth, "A" Battery,

Wounded at Fish Creek:—

Capt. Clarke, 90th; Capt. Wise, A. D. C.; Lieut. Doucett, A.D.C; Lieut. Bruce, M. I.; Capt. Gardner, M. I.; Private

C. F. King, M. I.; Private H. P. Porin, M. I.; Private
J. Langford, M. I.; Gunner Asseline, "A" Battery; Gunner
Emeye, "A" Battery; Bombardier Taylor, "A" Battery;
Sergeant-Major Mawhinney, "A" Battery; Driver Harrison;
Private H. P. Wilson; Private E. Mannsell; Private Walter
Woodman; Private R. H. Dunn, School of Infantry; Private
H. Jones, School of Infantry; Private R. Jones, School
of Infantry; Col.-Sergt. Cummings, School of Infantry;
Corporal Lethbridge, 90th; Private Kemp; Corporal Code;
Private Hartop; Private Blackwood; Private Canniff;
Private W. W. Matthews; Private Lovell; Private Cane,
10th Royals; Private Wheeeling, 10th Royals, knee
dislocated; Private Hislop, 90th; Private Chambers, 90th;
Corporal Thecker, 90th; Private Bouchette, 90th; Private
Swan 90th; Corporal Brown.

Killed at Battleford:—

Frank Smart, shot on picket.

Killed by Indians:—

John Walkinshaw and Albert Harkness.

Killings and Woundings elsewhere:—

Sergeant Snyder, injured by explosion at Peterboro; Lieut. Morrow, accidentally shot; Private Moberley, broken arm; Kelsey, Midland Battalion, jumped from train, probably lost; G. H. Douglass, injured by fall from horse; Marwich, Halifax Battalion, died from exposure, a member of the 9th (Quebec) Battalion, died from exposure; Farm Instructor Payne; Barnez Fremont, rancher, Achille Blois, 9th Quebec, died from fever.

Killed at Poundmaker's Reserve:—

Private Arthur Dobbs, Battleford Rifles; Bugler Foulks,
School of Infantry, Corporals Laurie and Sleight, and
Trumpeter Burke, Mounted Police; Privates Rogers and
Osgoode, Governor-General's Foot Guards; Tleamster Winder,
of Regina.

Wounded at Poundmaker's Reserve:—

Col-Sergt. Cooper, in the hip, Private G. Varey, in the shoulder, Private Lloyd, in the shoulder, and Private G. Watts, in the thigh, Queen's Own Rifles. Lieut. Pelletier, in the thigh, Sergt. Gaffney, in the arm, Corporal Morton, in the groin, and Gunner Reynolds, in the arm, "B" Battery. Sergt. Winters, in the face, Private McQuillan, in the side, Governor-General's

Foot Guards. Sergt. Ward, in the shoulder, Mounted Police. Sergt.-Major Spackman, in the arm, Bugler Gilbert, in the arm, Infantry School.

Killed at Batoche:—

Gunner Wm. Phillips, "A" Battery, Quebec; Private T, Moor, No. 3 company, Royal Grenadiers, Toronto; Capt. John French, scout; Capt. Brown, scout; Lieut. Fitch, 10th Royal Grenadiers, shot through the heart; W. P. Krippen, of Perth, a surveyor; Private Haidisty, 90th Winnipeg Battalion; Private Fraser, 90th Winnipeg Battalion. Of the foregoing the last six were killed on Monday, the first on Saturday, and Private Moor on Sunday.

Wounded at Batoche:—

Tenth Royal Grenadiers:—Major Dawson, slightly in the ankle, able to limp about; Capt. Manley slightly in the foot; Capt. Mason flesh wound in the thigh; Staff Sergt. T. M. Mitchell, slight wound in the eye; Private R. Cook in the arm; Private G. Barbour, slight scratch in the head; Private G. W, Quigley, flesh wound in the arm; Private J. Marshall in the calf; Private H. Wilson, slight wound across the back; Bugler, M. Vaughan, in the finger; Private Scovell, slight flesh wound; Private Stead, slight flesh wound; Private Cantwell.

The 90th Battalion:—Corp. Gillies, Sergt.-Major Watson, Private O. A. Wheeler, Private Young, Sergt. Jackes, Private M. Erickson, Private Kemp.

Surveyor Scouts:—Lieut Garden.

Capt. French's Scouts:—Trooper Cook.

"A" Battery:—Driver Jas. Stout, Gunner Fairbanks, Gunner Charpentier, Gunner Twohey.

Midland Battalion:—Lieut. Geo. Laidlaw, Lieut. Helliwell, Corp. Helliwell, Private Barton.

Meanwhile the campaign goes on, and we know not what tidings any day may bring forth. There is no use now in having long discussions as to whose shoulders should bear the responsibility of all the devastation, terror, misery and blood; the duty of the hour is to put an end to the Rebellion. Riel must be captured at any cost; so, too, must Dumont. Men so strongly a menace to public peace as Riel and his bad and fearless ally, Dumont, must not be given the opportunity again of covering the land with blood. There must be a pretty wholesome hanging in the North-West, and the gentlemen whom the authorities must give first attention to are the two villains just named, Poundmaker, Big Bear, Little Pine, Lucky Man, and those bloody wolves who perpetrated the butcheries at Frog Lake.

I have said that this is not the place to discuss at length the question of the Government's responsibility for this blood, and sorrow, and misery. Neither is it. Yet one and all believe, though thousands will belie their convictions, that there has been a criminal mismanagement of these half-breed people by the authorities at Ottawa.

I have been obliged to show that in the past, many of our French co-patriots bestowed a most astonishing and unjustifiable sympathy for Riel. I am glad to be able to say that in the present case, while censuring the Government for its indifference to the grievances of the half-breeds, they have no word of justification for the murderous apostle of tumult. Bishop Langevin, brother of the Hon the Minister of Public Works, issued a pastoral, in which there was no uncertain sound. He called upon the faithful sons of the country within his diocese to come forward and join hands against a cause of tumult, destruction and murder.

THE TRIAL AND EXECUTION OF LOUIS RIEL.

On the 20th of July the Court met, when Riel was formally arraigned, the clerk reading the long indictment. In reply to the interrogation whether the prisoner pled guilty to the charge of treason, his counsel rose and took exception to the jurisdiction of the Court. The plea entered by the defence was to the affect that the presiding stipendiary magistrate was incompetent to try a case involving the death penalty, and urged that Riel should be tried by one of the duly constituted courts in Ontario or in British Columbia. Mr. Christopher Robinson, Q.C., for the Crown, asked for an adjournment for eight days, to prepare a reply to the plea, which was granted. The Court then adjourned to the 28th instant.

On the re-opening of the Court, counsel expressed themselves ready to proceed. Only a few minutes were taken up in selecting a jury. Twelve persons were called, five of whom were peremptorily challenged by the defence, and one by the Crown. The remaining six were sworn in to try the prisoner at the bar. Their names are as follows: —H. J. Painter, E. Everett, E. J. Brooks, J. W. Merryfield, H. Dean, and F. Crosgrove. During the selection of the jury, it is observed by a correspondent of *The Mail*, to whom we shall be indebted for the reports of the trial, in making the present abstract, "that Riel anxiously watched the face of every man as he was selected and sworn, as though he could read their inmost thoughts as they took the oath."

After reading the indictment to the jury, Mr. B. B. Osler, Q.C., opened the case for the Crown, in which he explained the nature of the charge against the prisoner, whose career he traced through the successive steps of the rebellion, and indicated the weight and character of the evidence to be brought against its wicked instigator and chief leader. The plea of the defence of the incompetence of the Court to try the case, was first answered by the learned counsel, who remarked, that the character, and composition of the Court, as well as the provision for the trial of capital offences by a jury of six men instead of twelve, were in harmony with the Dominion Law enacted for the Government of the Territories, and that the Dominion Parliament had the right, under the British North America Act, to make that law. "The absence of the Grand Jury was explained, on the ground that such juries were essentially county organizations, and were impossible in large districts with small and scattered populations." The same reason explained the limiting of the jury to half the usual number. It was also stated that the Crown deemed it unwise, if indeed it were not impossible, to issue a Special Commission for the trial of the prisoner.

Mr. Osler proceeding said, that Riel not only aided and abetted the illegal acts of the rebels, but directed these acts.

"The testimony he claimed," says a writer in *The Illustrated War News*, "was abundantly sufficient to bring home to the prisoner his guilt in the charges against him. He (Mr. Osler) read the document in Riel's handwriting to Crozier, in which Riel threatened a war of extermination against the whites, and traced the prisoner's conduct afterwards to show that he had tried to carry out that threat. It was no constructive treason that was sought to be proved, but treason involving the shedding of brave men's blood. The accused had been led on, not by the desire to aid his friends in a lawful agitation for redress of a grievance, but by his inordinate vanity and desire for power and wealth."

"The first overt act of treason was committed," continued Mr. Osler, "when the French half-breeds were requested by Riel to bring their arms with them to a meeting to be held at Batoche on March 3rd. This indicated that the prisoner intended to resort to violence. On the 18th instant they find him (Riel) sending out armed men and taking prisoners, including Mr. Lash, the Indian agent of the St. Lament region, and others, also looting the stores at and near Batoche, stopping freighters and appropriating their freight. A few days later the French half-breeds were under arms, and were joined by the Indians of the neighbourhood, who were incited to rise by the prisoner. On the 21st inst. Major Crozier did all he could to get the armed men to disperse, but directed by Riel, they refused to do so, and taking their orders from him, they continued in rebellion. He held a document in his hands, in the prisoner's handwriting," added Mr. Osler, "which contained the terms on which Fort Carlton would be spared attack by the surrender and march out of Major Crozier and the mounted police. This document was never delivered, but was found with other papers in the rebel council chamber after the taking of Batoche. It was said in this notification to Crozier that the rebels would attack the police if they did not vacate Carlton, and would commence a war of extermination of the white race. This document was direct evidence of the treasonable intentions of the prisoner. Ten days previously Riel declared himself determined to rule or perish, and the declaration was followed by this demand. It would be said that, at last, when a clash of arms was imminent, Riel objected to forcible measures; but this document was a refutation of that assertion. At Duck Lake the prisoner had taken upon himself the responsibility of ordering his men to fire on the police. At Fish Creek, if Riel was not there, he directed the movement, and was therefore responsible. On the day of the fight he went back to Batoche to finish the rifle-pits. In the contest at Batoche the prisoner was seen bearing arms, and giving such directions as would show that he was the main mover. His treatment of the prisoners, his letters to

Middleton, and other documents would show Riel's leadership. A letter found in Poundmaker's camp would show his deliberate intention of bringing on this country the calamity of an Indian war. All this would be proven, and it would be shown that the prisoner had not come here to aid his friends in the redress of grievances, but in order to use the half-breeds for his own selfish ends." Mr. Osler closed with a reference to the death and suffering which had been caused by the ambition of one man, and impressed upon the jury the grave responsibility they were charged with in bringing his crime home to the prisoner.

The first witness called by the Crown was DR. WILLOUGHBY, of SASKATOON. After having been sworn, witness said that the prisoner had stated to him that the Fort Garry trouble, when Scott had been shot, was nothing to what was going to take place. He said that the Indians only waited for him to strike the first blow to join him, and that he had the United States at his back. He seemed greatly excited, and said:—"It is time, doctor, that the breeds should assert their rights, and it will be well for those who have lived good lives." A party of armed men then drove up, and Riel said, pointing to them, "My people intend striking a blow for their rights. They have petitioned the Government over and over again, the only reply being an increase of the police force each time." The Indians, he said, had arranged their plans, and when the first blow was struck they would be joined by the American Indians. They would issue a proclamation, and assert that the time had arrived for him to rule the country or perish in the attempt. He promised to divide the country into seven equal portions, one of which was to be the new Ireland of the new North-West. He said the rebellion of fifteen years ago was not a patch on what this would be.

THOS. McKAY, a loyal half-breed, was next called, who testified that he joined the Volunteer contingent from Prince Albert which formed part of Major Crozier's command at Duck Lake. Previous to that engagement he accompanied Mr. Hillyard Mitchell in his mission to Batoche, where the rebels had their headquarters. His object in going to Batoche was to point cut to the French half-breeds the danger they were getting into in taking up arms. On arriving at the village he was met by an armed guard who conducted him, with Mr. Mitchell, to the rebel council room, where he was introduced to Riel "as one of Her Majesty's soldiers." We here quote part of the examination, by Mr. Christopher Robinson, of this Witness.

Q.—Who introduced you to the prisoner?

A.—Mr. Mitchell introduced me to Mr. Riel as one of Her Majesty's soldiers.

Q.—That is Mr. Hillyard Mitchell?

A.—Yes. I shook hands with Mr. Riel and had a talk with him. I said, "There appears be great excitement here, Mr. Riel." He said, "No, there is no excitement at all; it was simply that the people were trying to redress their grievances, as they had asked repeatedly for their rights; that they had decided to make a demonstration." I told him it was a very dangerous thing to resort to arms. He said he had been waiting fifteen long years and that they had been imposed upon, and it was time now, after they had waited patiently that their rights should be given, as the poor half-breeds had been imposed upon. I disputed his wisdom and advised him to adopt different measures.

Q.—Did he speak of himself at all in the matter?

A.—He accused me of having neglected my people. He said if it was not for men like me their grievances would have been redressed long ago, that as no one took an interest in these people he had decided to take the lead in the matter.

Q.—Well?

A.—He accused me of neglecting them. I told him it was simply a matter of opinion, that I had certainly taken an interest in them, and my interest in the country was the same as theirs, and that I had advised them time and again, and that I had not neglected them. I also said that he had neglected them a long time if he took as deep an interest as he professed to. He became very excited, and got up and said, "You don't know what we are after—it is blood, blood; we want blood; it is a war of extermination. Everybody that is against us is to be driven out of the country." There were two curses in the country—the Government and the Hudson Bay Co. He further said the first blood they wanted was mine. There were some little dishes on the table, and he got hold of a spoon and said, "You have no blood, you are a traitor to your people, your blood is frozen, and all the little blood you have will be there in five minutes"—putting the spoon up to my face, and pointing to it. I said, "If you think you are benefiting your cause by taking my blood, you are quite welcome to it." He called his people and the committee, and wanted to put me on trial for my life, and Garnot got up and went to the table with a sheet of paper, and Gabriel Dumont took a chair on a syrup keg, and Riel called up the witnesses against me.

At this juncture Riel was called away to attend a committee meeting of the rebel government. Subsequently, by the mediation of Hillyard Mitchell, Riel's wrath at McKay was placated, and he was allowed to return to Fort Carlton with his intercessor. Before leaving, Riel apologized to McKay for what he had said to him, and asked him to join the insurgents, which witness, of course, would not do, being a loyal half-breed and a volunteer in the ranks of the Prince Albert contingent with Crozier at Fort Carlton.

McKay then detailed the incidents of the disastrous engagement with the rebels at Duck Lake, and gave strong testimony to criminate Riel, which the counsel for the defence utterly failed to shake.

The next witness WAS JOHN ASTLEY, surveyor of PRINCE ALBERT, who was long prisoner of Riel's at Batoche, and the rebel chief's messenger on the day of the taking of the village by the loyal forces under Middleton. The witness gave a vivid description of his capture and imprisonment by Riel, and his subsequent release by the volunteers at Batoche. Riel acknowledged to him that he ordered his men in the name of the Almighty to fire at Duck Lake. He did not do so, however until, as he thought, the police had fired. Riel told him he must have another fight with the soldiers to secure better terms of surrender from Gen. Middleton.

SECOND DAY OF THE TRIAL.

The second day of the Riel trial brought out sufficient evidence to incriminate the prisoner, and to lead the Crown prosecutors to waive the calling of other witnesses. During the proceedings the prisoner, it is reported, manifested more interest than he did on the first day of the trial, and his dark penetrating eye restlessly wandered from witness to counsel, and from bench to jury. "All day long a couple of medical men sat watching his actions, to discover, if possible, whether his mind was affected or not." His disagreement with his counsel towards the close of the day, caused an exciting break in the proceedings.

GEORGE KERR, of Kerr Brothers, BATOCHE, was the first witness sworn. He testified that on the 18th of March, Riel, with some fifty armed half-breeds, came to his store, and demanded, and obtained, all his guns and ammunition. His store was sacked, and later on he was himself taken prisoner, but was subsequently released. Riel, he testified, directed the rebel movements in concert with Gabriel Dumont.

HARRY WALTERS, another storekeeper at BATOCHE, was then examined, and gave similar testimony as to the sacking of his store, and of Riel's demand for arms and ammunition. On his refusing to accede to the demand of the prisoner and the breeds with him, Riel said, "You had better do it quietly. If we succeed, I will pay you; if not, the Dominion Government will." I refused, said Walters, and they forced themselves in and took the arms. I was arrested shortly after. Riel said the movement was for the freedom of the people. The country, if they succeeded, was to be divided, giving a seventh to the half-breeds, a seventh to the Indians, a seventh to church and schools, the remainder to be Crown Lands. I was kept prisoner three days, being liberated by Riel. Riel said, God was with their people, and that if the whites ever struck a blow, a thunderbolt would destroy them. They took everything out of my store before morning, the prisoner superintending the removal of the goods.

HILLYARD MITCHELL sworn, was examined by Mr. Osler. He said—I am an Indian trader, have a store at Duck Lake; heard there was an intention by rebels to take my store. I went to Fort Carlton and saw Major Crozier on the Thursday prior to the Duck Lake fight; saw prisoner on that Thursday at Batoche. Saw some people at the river armed. At the village I saw some English half-breed freighters who had been taken prisoners by Riel, and their freight also taken. Philip Garnot took me to the priest's house. I saw the prisoner there with Charles Nolin, Guardupuy and others. I think this was on the 19th of March. I told Riel that I had come to give some advice to the half-breeds. Riel said the Government had always answered their demands by sending more police. They were willing to fight 500 police. He said he had been trampled on and kept out of the country, and he would bring the Government and Sir Jonn Macdonald to their knees.

THOMAS E. JACKSON was next examined by Mr. Osler, and deposed that he was a druggist, at Prince Albert, and a brother of Wm. Henry Jackson, an insane prisoner of Riel's. Riel, witness testified, asked him to write to the eastern papers, placing a favourable construction on his (Riel's) actions. Riel had made an application to Government for $35,000 as indemnity for loss of property; he showed the greatest hatred to the English, and his motives were those of revenge for ill-treatment at the time of the Red River rebellion. Having questioned Riel's present motives and plans, witness was taken prisoner and placed in close confinement. Riel afterwards accused me of having advised an English half-breed to desert. When Middleton was attacking Batoche, Riel came to witness and told him if Middleton killed any of their women and children he would massacre the prisoners. He wrote a message to Middleton to that effect, and I carried it to the General. (The message was produced and identified by witness). I did not return to the rebel camp. Saw the prisoner armed once after the Fish Creek fight. Riel was in command at Batoche, Dumont being in immediate command of the men. I know prisoner's handwriting. (The original summons to Major Crozier to surrender, the letter to Crozier asking him to come and take away the dead after Duck Lake fight, a letter to "dear relatives" at Fort Qu'Appelle, a letter to the half-breeds and Indians about Battleford, a letter to Poundmaker, and other documents were put in and identified by witness as being in Riel's handwriting).

Cross-examined by Mr. Fitzpatrick—The agitation was for provincial rights and their claims under the Manitoba treaty, and I was in sympathy with it. Riel was brought into the country by the French half-breeds. I attended a meeting at Prince Albert immediately after Riel's arrival in June, 1884. Riel said what they wanted was a constitutional agitation, and if they could not accomplish their ends in five years they would take ten to do it. Riel was their adviser; was not a member of the Executive Committee. Up to March last, from all I heard prisoner say or discovered otherwise, I believed Riel meant simply a constitutional agitation, as was being carried on by the other settlers. Riel had told him the priests were opposed to him, and that they were all wrong. Heard Riel talk of dividing up the country to be bestowed on the half-breeds, Poles, Hungarians, Bavarians, etc. When I was Riel's prisoner I heard him talk of this division, which I thought meant a division of the proceeds of sale of lands in a scheme of immigration. This was altogether different from what he had all along proposed at the meetings.

All the documents Riel signed that I know of were signed "Exovide" (one of the flock). Riel explained that his new religion was a liberal form of Roman Catholicism, and that the Pope had no power in Canada. Think Riel wanted to exercise the power of the Pope himself. These expressions were made by Riel after the rebellious movement was begun.

GENERAL MIDDLETON was now called, and was examined by Mr. C. Robinson, Q.C. He testified that he was sent by the Minister of Militia to quell the outbreak on the Saskatchewan, and gave the well-known details of his encounter with the rebels at Fish Creek, and of his subsequent movement on Batoche. He testified to receiving two letters from Riel on the day of the capture of Batoche, in one of which Riel threatened to massacre the prisoners in his possession if he (Middleton) fired upon the half-breed women and children. The letter was produced in Court, and identified by the General.

CAPT. GEO. H. YOUNG, of the Winnipeg Field Battery, deposed that he was present at Batoche as Brigade Major under the last witness, and was in the charge at the close. Witness was first in the rebel council chamber after the capture of the village, and found and took possession of the rebel archives. A number of documents were produced, which witness recognised as those he had secured. After Riel's surrender he was given into witness's custody and taken to Regina.

MAJOR JARVIS, in command of the Winnipeg Field Battery during the campaign, and to whom the charge of the papers found at Batoche was confided, identified the papers produced in Court.

MAJOR CROZIER, of the N.-W. Mounted Police, was next sworn, and detailed the fact that he was met by an armed force of rebels at Duck Lake and fired upon, losing many of his command in killed and wounded. He testified that, subsequent to this engagement, a man named Sanderson brought him a letter from Riel asking him to come and remove his dead from the field.

CHARLES NOLIN was next called, and was examined by Mr. Casgrain in French. The deposition of this witness we take from the Toronto *Globe*. Nolin deposed that he lived in St. Laurent and formerly in Manitoba. He knew when Riel came to this country in July, 1884. And met him many times. Riel showed him a book he had written in which he said he would destroy England, and also Rome and the Pope. Riel spoke to him of his plans in December, expressing his wish for money, a sum between ten and fifteen thousand dollars. Riel had no plan to get it, but he wanted to claim an indemnity from the Dominion Government; that they owed him $100,000. Riel told him he had had an interview with Father Andre, and at that time he was at open war with the clergy, but had made peace with

Father Andre in order to gain his ends. Riel went into the church with Father Andre and other priests, and promised to do nothing against them, and Father Andre had promised to use his influence with the Government to secure an indemnity of $35,000. This was in the beginning of December, 1884, the agreement being made at St. Laurent. Between December and February 14th, witness had taken part in seven meetings. Riel said if he could get the money from the Government he would go wherever the Government would send him—to the Province of Quebec or elsewhere. Otherwise, he said, before the grass was very long, they would see foreign armies in Canada. He would begin with subduing Manitoba, and afterwards turn against the North-West. Prisoner afterwards prepared to go to the United States, and told the people it would look well if they attempted to prevent him from going. Riel never had the intention of leaving the country, but wanted witness to get the people to tell him not to go. Witness was chairman of a meeting which was held, and brought the matter up. On the 2nd March a meeting was held at the settlement between Riel and Father Andre. There were seven or eight half-breeds there. Prisoner appeared to be very excited, and told Father Andre he must give him permission to proclaim a Provisional Government before 12 o'clock. On the 3rd March a meeting was held for the English half-breeds. About forty armed French-half-breeds came there. Riel spoke and said the police wanted to arrest him, but he had the real police. Witness spoke also at the meeting on the 5th of March. Riel afterwards told witness he had decided to take up arms and induce the people to take up arms for the glory of God, the good of the Church, and the saving of their souls. About twenty days before the prisoner took up arms witness broke entirely from him. On the 19th witness was made prisoner by four of Riel's men and taken to the church, where he found some half-breeds and Indians armed. That night he was taken before the council and was acquitted. Riel protested against the decision. Witness was condemned to death, and he was thus forced to join the rebels to save his life. The conditions of surrender to Crozier were put in his hands to be delivered to Crozier, but he did not deliver the letter. Riel was present at the Duck Lake fight, on the 26th March, and was one of the first to go out to meet the police, carrying a cross in his hands.

Cross examined by Mr. Lemieux.—I have taken an active part in political affairs of the country. In 1869 I was in Manitoba. In 1884 Riel was living in Montana with his wife and children. I participated in the movement to bring Riel here; believed Riel would be of advantage in obtaining redress of the grievances. The clergy had not taken part in the political movement, but had assisted them in obtaining their rights. They thought it was necessary to have Riel as a point to rally round. Delegates were sent to invite Riel to come, and he came with his wife and family. A constitutional political movement was made, in which the half-breeds of all creeds took part, and the whites, though they were not active promoters, were sympathizers. Did not believe Riel ever wanted to return to Montana, although he spoke of it. After the Government refused to grant the indemnity to Riel witness did not believe he would be useful as a constitutional leader. It was after the indemnity was refused that Riel spoke of going away. Witness denied that in 1869 he started an agitation with Riel, and then, as in the present case, abandoned him. He only went as far as was constitutional. He had heard prisoner say he considered himself a prophet, and said he had inspiration in his liver and in every other part of his body. He wrote upon a piece of paper that he was inspired. He showed witness a book written with buffalo blood, which was a plan that after Riel had taken England and Canada, Quebec was to be given to the Prussians, Ontario to the Irish, and the North-West to be divided among the various nationalities of Europe, the Jews, Hungarians, and Bavarians included. The rebel council had first condemned witness to death, and afterwards liberated him, and he accepted a position in the council in order to save his life. Witness said that whenever the word police was mentioned Riel became very excited, having heard that the Government had answered their petitions for redress by sending 500 extra police.

At this part of the cross-examination of Nolin, the proceedings were interrupted by an excited clamour of Riel, to be allowed to interrogate the prisoner, and to assist personally in the conduct of his case. This the Court could only allow with the consent of prisoner's counsel. His counsel objected, and urged that such a proceeding would prejudice their client's case; but Riel persisted, and the rest of the day was wasted in fruitless altercation, which neither the Court nor the counsel for the Crown could allay. The chief cause of Riel's excitement seemed to be the determination of his counsel to press the plea of insanity, a plea which, throughout the trial, Riel strongly objected to be urged on his behalf. The Court in the midst of the altercation, adjourned.

THIRD DAY OF THE TRIAL.

[Footnote: In preparing this abstract of the day's proceedings, the writer acknowledges to have drawn from the reports published in the Toronto *Globe* and *Mail*, and the Montreal *Gazette* And *Star*.]

The Riel trial was resumed at Regina, on the morning of July 30th, by MR. GREEN SHIELDS' addressing the jury for the defence. The Court-room was again filled to its utmost capacity. After referring to the difficulty counsel had met, in the prisoner's endeavour to obstruct their conduct of the case, Mr. Greenshields dwelt upon the history of the Indians and half-breeds in the North-West Territories, pointing out their rights to the soil. In this Court they had a different procedure from that in other parts of the Dominion, and while not desiring to be understood that the prisoner would not receive as fair a trial as the machinery provided made possible, he questioned whether a jury of six men, nominated by the presiding magistrate, was sufficient to satisfy the demands of Magna Charta,—the great bulwark of the rights and liberties of all British subjects. He believed any of the older Provinces would rebel against such an encroachment on their rights, and he did not see why such a condition of things should obtain here. For years the half-breeds had been making futile efforts to obtain their rights. All these efforts had been met by rebuffs, or had received no attention whatever from the Federal Government, and those very rights for which the half-breeds were supplicating and petitioning were being handed over to railway corporations, colonization companies, and like concerns. He would not say that the action of the Government justified armed rebellion—the shedding of blood—but it left in these poor people those smouldering fires of discontent that were so easily fanned into rebellion by a madman such as Riel. The prisoner had been invited by the half-breeds to come among them from a foreign country to assist them in making a proper representation of their grievances to the Government. They were unlettered and required an active sympathizer, with education sufficient to properly conduct the agitation. Riel was the man they chose, and there was no evidence to show that when Riel came to this country he came with any intention of inciting the people to armed rebellion. His work was begun and carried on up till January in a perfectly constitutional manner. After that time, as the jury had seen in the cross-examination of the witnesses for the prosecution, no effort was made by the defence to deny that overt acts of treason had been committed in the presence of the prisoner; but evidence would be brought to show that at the time these acts were countenanced by the prisoner, he was of unsound mind and not responsible for what he did. The peculiar disease of the prisoner was called by men learned in diseases of the mind, "megalomania." This species of mental disease developed two delusions—one the desire for and belief that the patient could obtain great power in political matters to rule or govern, another his desire to found a great church. That the prisoner was possessed of these delusions, the evidence abundantly proved. The jury might consider, with some grounds for the belief, that the evidence of Charles Nolin, who swore that the prisoner was willing to leave the country if he obtained from the Government a gratuity of $35,000, was inconsistent with the real existence of such a monomania as the prisoner was afflicted with. But not one isolated portion, but the whole, of Nolin's evidence should be considered. Other portions of his testimony, for instance, prisoner's opinions on religious matters, and his intention to divide up the country between various foreign nationalities, were conclusive proof of the prisoner's insanity. This was a great State trial, the speaker said, and he warned the jury to throw aside the influence of heated public opinion, as it was expressed at present. There were many people executed for having taken part in the rebellion of 1837, and it was questionable if there could be found anyone now who would justify those executions. The beat of private feeling had died away, and the jury should be careful that no hasty conclusion in this case should leave posterity a chance to say that their verdict had been a wrong one. They should, if possible, look at the case with the calmness of the historian, throwing aside all preconceived notions of the case that interfered with the evidence given in the Court, and build up their verdict on the testimony brought out here. In the course of his remarks, Mr. Greenshields said, that he accused no Government in particular for neglecting the claims of the breeds; but if the authorities had paid attention to the petitions which had been addressed to them, the rebellion would never have occurred. He paid a glowing tribute to the volunteers, who left their private occupations and came from all parts of the Dominion to suppress the outbreak.

At the conclusion of Mr. Greenshield's address, FATHER ANDRE, Superior of the Oblat Fathers in the district of Carlton, was called for the defence. He said he had been intimately associated with the breeds for a quarter of a century. Riel had been induced to come to this country by the settlers to assist them. The witness had a thorough knowledge of what was going on amongst the settlers. He had no knowledge of petitions having been sent to the Government during the agitation; but he had himself indirectly communicated with the Government last December, with the object of getting the prisoner out of the country. The pretensions or claims of the breeds changed frequently. After Riel's arrival the Government had been notified three or four times of what was transpiring. The Government had promised to take the matter into consideration. The Government had replied to one petition by telegram, conceding the old survey. This was an important concession. At Batoche three scrips had been issued, and at Duck Lake forty were given. The witness never liked talking with the prisoner on religion or politics. On these subjects Riel's language frightened the witness, who considered him undoubtedly crazy on these subjects, while on all other points he was sane enough. Once, at a meeting of priests, the advisability of allowing such a man to perform religious duties was discussed, and it was unanimously agreed that the man was insane. The discussion of religious or political subjects with him was like dangling a red flag in front of a bull.

PHILIP GARNEAU, of Batoche, but at present a prisoner in Regina gaol, was now sworn and deposed as follows:—I saw Riel at Batoche last fall; had seen him several times before January. During the trouble I talked with him at my house on religious matters. He said the spirit of Elias, the prophet, was in him. He wanted the people to believe that. He often said the Spirit of God told him to do this or that. During his stay at my house Riel prayed aloud all night; never heard such prayers before; prisoner must have made them up. He could not stand to be contradicted, and was very irritable. Heard him declare he was representing St. Peter. Heard him talking of the country being divided into seven Provinces, and he was going to bring in seven different nationalities to occupy them. I did not believe he would succeed in that. He expected the assistance of the Jews and other nationalities, to whom he was going to award a Province each for their aid. Riel said he was sure to succeed, it was a divine mission, and God was the chief of the movement; only met him once before the trouble. I thought the man was crazy.

Cross-examined by Mr. Robinson—I followed Riel solely because he forced me with armed men. He had great influence over the half-breeds, who listened to and followed his advice,

FATHER FOURMAND sworn, examined by Mr. Lemieux in French—I am a priest of St. Laurent; went there in 1875. Have had conversations with Riel since the time of the rebellion. Often conversed with him on political and religious subjects. I was present at the meeting of priests at which Riel's sanity was questioned. I knew the facts upon which the question arose. Before the rebellion Riel was a polite and pleasant man to me. When he was not contradicted about political affairs he was quiet, but when opposed he was violent. As soon as the rebellion commenced he lost all control of himself, and threatened to burn all the churches. He believed there was only one God; that Christ the Son was not God, neither was the Holy Ghost, and in consequence the Virgin Mary was not the mother of God, but of the Son of God. He changed the song beginning "Hail Mary, mother of God," to "Hail Mary, mother of the Son of God." He denied the real presence of

God in the Host, it was a man of six feet. Riel said he was going to Quebec, France and Italy, and would overthrow the Pope and choose a Pope or appoint himself. We finally concluded there was no other way of explaining his conduct than that he was insane. Noticed a great change in prisoner as the agitation progressed. When the fathers opposed him he attacked them. Witness was brought before the rebel council by the prisoner, to give an account of his conduct. He called me a little tiger, being very excited. Never showed me a book of his prophecies written in buffalo blood, although I heard of it.

Cross-examined by Mr. Casgrain—Most of the half-breeds followed Riel in his religious views; some opposed them. The prisoner was relatively sane before the rebellion. The prisoner proclaimed the rebellion on March 18th. I promised to occupy a position of neutrality towards the provisional Government. He could better explain prisoner's conduct on the ground of insanity than that of great criminality. Witness naturally had a strong friendship towards the prisoner.

The afternoon was devoted to expert testimony respecting the prisoner's sanity.

MEDICAL TESTIMONY.

DR. ROY, of the Beauport Asylum, Quebec, said the prisoner was an inmate of that institution for nineteen months. He was discharged in January, 1878. He suffered from ambitious mania. One of the distinguishing characteristics of that form of insanity is that, so long as the particular hobby is not touched, the patient appears perfectly sane. From what he heard the witnesses say, and from the prisoner's actions yesterday, he had no hesitation in pronouncing the man insane, and he believed him not to be responsible for his acts.

DR. CLARKE, of Toronto, was the next witness. He said he was the Superintendent of the Toronto Lunatic Asylum. He has had nine or ten years' experience in treating lunatics. He examined the prisoner twice yesterday and once this morning. From what evidence he had heard and from his own examination, provided the witnesses told the truth and the prisoner was not malingering, there was no doubt of his being insane.

Cross-examined by Mr. Osler—It is impossible for any man to say that a person like Riel, who is sharp and well-educated, is either insane or sane. He (the witness) would require to have him under his notice for months to form an opinion. The man's actions are consistent with fraud. Thinks he knows the difference between right and wrong, subject to his delusion.

DR. WALLACE was next called. He said he was Superintendent of the Insane Asylum at Hamilton. He had listened to the evidence in this case. He saw the prisoner alone for half an hour. He has formed the opinion that there is no indication of insanity about him. He thinks the prisoner knows the difference between right and wrong. The person suffering from megalomania often imagines he is a king, divinely inspired, has the world at his feet—supreme egotism in fact. It is one of the complications of paralytic insanity.

DR. JUKES, of the Mounted Police, would not say the prisoner was not insane. He had seen him daily since May, and noticed no traces of insanity.

The Court adjourned at five o'clock.

RIEL'S ADDRESS TO THE JURY.

At the outset, writes W. A. H., correspondent of the Montreal *Star*, Riel spoke in a quiet and low tone, many of his statements carrying home conviction to his hearers. "At any rate," was the subsequent comment, "Riel speaks with the belief that he is right." Gradually as he proceeded and got fairly launched into his subject, his eyes sparkled, his body swayed to and fro as if strongly agitated, and his hands accomplished a series of wonderful gestures as he warmed up and spoke with impassioned eloquence. His hearers were spell-bound, and well they might, as each concluding assertion with terrible earnestness was uttered with the effect and force of a trumpet blast. That every soul in Court was impressed is not untrue, and many ladies were moved to tears. The following is an epitome of what he said:—

"Your Honour, and gentlemen of the jury—It would be an easy matter for me to-day, to play the *role* of a lunatic, because the circumstances are such as to excite any ordinary man subject to natural excitement after what has transpired to-day. The natural excitement, or may I add anxiety, which my trial causes me is enough to justify me in acting in the manner of a demented man; but I hope, with the help of God, that I will maintain a calm exterior and act with the decorum that suits this honourable Court. You have, no doubt, seen by the papers produced by the Crown, that I was not a man disposed to think of God at the beginning. Gentlemen, I don't want to play the part of a lunatic.

"Oh, my God, help me through the grace and divine influence of Jesus. Oh, my God bless me, bless this Court, bless this jury, and bless my good lawyers, who at great sacrifice have came nearly 700 leagues to defend me. Bless the lawyers for the Crown, for they have done what they considered their duty. God grant that fairness be shown. Oh, Jesus, change the curiosity of the ladies and others here to sanctity. The day of my birth I was helpless, and my mother was helpless. Somebody helped her. I lived, and although a man I am as helpless to-day as I was a babe on my mother's breast. But the North-West is also my mother: although the North-West is sick and confined, there is some one to take care of her. I am sure that my mother will not kill me after forty-years life. My mother cannot take my life. She will be indulgent and will forget.

"When I came here from Montana, in July, 1884, I found the Indians starving. The state of affairs was terrible. The half-breeds were subsisting on the rotten pork of the Hudson Bay Company. This was the condition, this was the pride, of responsible Government! What did Louis Riel do? I did not equally forget the whites. I directed my attention to assist all classes, irrespective of creed, colour or nationality. We have made petitions to the Canadian Government, asking them to relieve the state of affairs. We took time. Those who know me, know we took time with the object of uniting all classes, even if I may speak it, all parties. Those who know me know I have suffered. I tried to come to an understanding with the authorities on different points. I believe I have done my duty. It was said that I was egotistical. A man cannot generalize himself unless he is imputed with the taint. After the Canadian Government, through the honourable under-secretary of state, replied to my letter regarding the half-breeds, then, and not till then, did I look after my private affairs. A good deal can be said of the distribution of land. I don't know if my dignity would permit me to mention what you term my foreign policy, but if I was allowed to explain or question certain witnesses, those things would have looked different. My lawyers are good, but they don't understand the circumstances. Be it understood that I appreciate their services. Were I to go into details, I could safely say what Captain Young has told you regarding my mission, to bring about practical results. I have writings; my career, is perhaps nearly run, but after dissolution my spirit will still bring about practical results."

Striking his breast he added:

"No one need say that the North-West is not suffering. The Saskatchewan was especially afflicted, but what have I done to bring about practical results? For ten years I have been aware that I had a mission to perform; now what encourages me is the fact that I still have a mission to perform. God is with me, He is in this dock, and God is with my lawyers, the same as he was with me in the battles of the Saskatchewan. I have not assumed my mission. In Manitoba, to-day, I have a mission to perform. To-day I am forgotten by the Manitobans as dead. Did I not obtain for that province a constitutional government notwithstanding the opposition of the Ottawa authorities? That was the cause of my banishment."

I thank the glorious General Middleton for his testimony that I possess my mental faculties. I felt that God was blessing me when those words were pronounced. I was in Beauport Asylum; Dr. Roy over there knows it, but I thank the Crown for destroying his testimony. I was in the Lunatic Asylum at Longue Pointe, near Montreal, also; and would like to see my old friends, Dr. Lachapelle and Dr. Howard, who treated me so charitably. Even if I am to die, I will have the satisfaction of knowing that I will not be regarded by all men as an insane person.

TO THE COURT.—"Your honour and gentlemen of the jury, my reputation, my life, my liberty, are in your hands, and are at your discretion. I am so confident in your high sense of duty that I have no anxiety as to the verdict. My calmness does not arise from the presumption that you will acquit me. Although you are only half a jury, only a shred of that proud old British constitution, I respect you. I can only trust, Judge and gentlemen, that good and practical results will arise from your judgment conscientiously rendered. I would call your attention to one or two points. The first is that the House of Commons, Senate and Ministry, which make the laws, do not respect the interests of the North-West. My second point is that the North-West Council has the defect of its parent. There are practically no elections, and it is a sham legislature."

Then, as if wandering from his subject, Riel broke forth and said:

"I was ready at Batoche; I fired and wounded your soldiers. Bear in mind, is my crime, committed in self-defence, so enormous? Oh, Jesus Christ! help me, for they are trying to tear me into pieces. Jurors, if you support the plea of insanity, otherwise acquit me all the same. Console yourselves with the reflection that you will be doing justice to one who has suffered for fifteen years, to my family, and to the North-West."

Riel concluded as follows, his language containing a strange admixture of the words applied to him by the medical experts, which he ingeniously turned against the Government:

"Your honours and gentlemen of the jury:—I am taking the circumstances of my trial as they are. The only thing to which I would respectfully call your attention before you retire to deliberate is the irresponsibility of the Government. It is a fact that the Government possesses an absolute lack of responsibility, an insanity complicated with analysis. A monster of irresponsible, insane government, and its little North-West council, had made up their minds to answer my petitions by surrounding me, and by suddenly attempting to jump at me and my people in the fertile valley of the Saskatchewan. You are perfectly justified in declaring that having my reason and sound mind, I acted reasonably and in self-defence, while the Government, my aggressor, being irresponsible, and consequently insane, cannot but have acted madly and wrong; and if high treason there is, it must be on its side, not on my part."

At the conclusion of Riel's lengthy address, MR. CHRISTOPHER ROBINSON, Q.C., closed the case for the Crown in a powerful speech, which went far to counteract the sympathetic effect produced by Riel's disconnected but eloquent oration. Mr. Robinson pointed out that no evidence was produced to show that the prisoner had not committed the acts he was charged with. From the evidence it was quite clear the prisoner was neither a patriot nor a lunatic. If prisoner was not responsible for the rebellion, who was? The speaker went over the evidence and showed that Riel's acts were not those of a lunatic, but well considered in all their bearings, and the deliberate acts of a particularly sound mind. The evidence as to Riel's confinement in an asylum nine years ago was not satisfactory. Why was he sent there under an assumed name? Why was the record of his case not produced along with the other papers, and a statement of his condition when leaving the asylum? Medical men were not always the best judges of insanity. Taking up the evidence against the prisoner, Mr. Robinson went over it in detail, and said no mercy should be shown one who had committed such acts. He pictured the terrible results if Riel had succeeded in his effort to rouse the Indians, The reason the prisoners Poundmaker and Big Bear had not been put in the witness box, was that they could not be asked to give evidence that would incriminate themselves.

MR. JUSTICE RICHARDSON then read over the evidence to the jury, after which the court adjourned.

THIRD DAY'S PROCEEDINGS.

[Footnote: This abstract of the final day's proceedings we take from the Toronto *Mail*.]

The court resumed its sittings on the morning of the 1st of August, at the usual hour, and Col. Richardson continued his charge to the jury He read all the principal evidence, commenting thereon, and finally charged the jury to do their duty without fear or favour.

THE VERDICT.

When the jury returned with the verdict at 3.15 p.m., after exactly one hour's deliberation, the prisoner, who had been on his knees in the dock praying incessantly, rose and stood facing the six men who came in bearing for him the message of life or death.

The CLERK of the Court, amid a silence so intense that, like the darkness of Egypt, it could be felt, asked if the gentlemen of the jury had agreed upon their verdict?

MR. COSGROVE, the foreman, answered in a low tone, but heard distinctly in the general hush, "We have!"

The CLERK then asked: "Is the prisoner guilty or not guilty?"

Everyone but the prisoner seemed anxious. He alone of all those present, eager to hear the message of fate, was calm.

The Foreman replied: "Guilty, with a recommendation to mercy!"

Riel smiled as if the sentence in no way affected him, and bowed gracefully to the jury.

THE PRISONER'S SPEECH.

COL. RICHARDSON asked the prisoner if he had anything to say why the sentence of the Court should not be passed upon him?

RIEL replied: Yes, your honour. Then he began, in a low, calm voice to detail the story of the half-breeds in Manitoba, and spoke at length of the rebellion of '69. He said that if he had to die for what had taken place, it would be a consolation to his wife and to his friends to know that he had not died in vain. In years to come people will look at Manitoba and say that Riel helped the dwellers of those fertile plains to obtain the benefits they now enjoy. He said it would be an easy thing for him to make an incendiary speech, but he would refrain. He said that God had given him a mission to perform, and if suffering was part of that mission, he bowed respectfully to the Divine will, and he was ready to accept the task, even if the end should be death. Like David, he had suffered, but he lacked two years of the time that David suffered. The prisoner then went into the history of the Red River rebellion at great length. He claimed that he had ruled the country for two months for the Government, and his only reward was a sentence of exile. The troubles in the Saskatchewan, he said, were but a continuation of the troubles of the Red River, and the breeds feel that they are being robbed by the Government, which has failed to carry out the treaty promises that had been made to them. The breeds sustained their rights in '69 by arms, and the people of Manitoba are enjoying the results to-day. The people of Saskatchewan only followed the same precedent, and he trusted that the same results would follow. He then spoke at great length of the part played by Sir John Macdonald, Sir George Cartier, and Bishop Tache in the Red River rebellion. The money that had been given to him and to Lepine on leaving the country had been accepted, he said, as part of what was justly their due. The whites were gradually crowding out the Indians and the Metis, and what was more natural and just than for them to take up arms in defence of their rights? He justified his claims to $35,000 by saying that it was offered to him to keep out of the country for three years. The English constitution, he said, had been perfected for the happiness of the world, and his wish to have the representatives of the different nations here was to give people from the countries of the Old World an opportunity of enjoying the blessings God had given England. God had given England great glory, but she must work for that glory or it would surely pass away. The Roman Empire was four hundred years in declining from its proud pre-eminence, and England would be in the same position; but before England faded away a grander England would be built up in this immense country. His heart, while it beat, would not abandon the idea of having a new Ireland, a new Germany, a new France here; and the people of those countries would enjoy liberties under the British constitution which they did not obtain at home. If he must die for his principles, if the brave men who were with him must die, he hoped the French-Canadians would come and help the people to get back what was being unjustly wrenched from them. Peace had always been uppermost in his thoughts, and it was to save the country from being deluged with blood later on that they strove for their rights now. He concluded by objecting to the jury and the decision of the Court, and asked that he be not tried for the alleged offences of this season, but that his whole career be put on trial, and the jury asked to give a decision as to whether his life and acts have in any way benefited the country or not.

THE SENTENCE.

Mr. CHRISTOPHER ROBINSON moved for the sentence of the Court.

Judge RICHARDSON then said: "Louis Riel, you are charged with treason. You let loose the flood gates of rapine and bloodshed, and brought ruin and death to many families, who, if let alone, were in comfort and a fair way of affluence. For what you did you have been given a fair and impartial trial. Your remarks are no excuse for your acts. You committed acts that the law demands an account for at your hands. The jury coupled with their verdict a recommendation to mercy. I can hold out no prospect for you, and I would recommend you to make your peace with God. For me, only one duty and a painful one to perform remains. It is to pass sentence upon you. If your life is spared, no one will feel more gratified than myself, but I can hold out no hope. The sentence of this Court upon you, Louis Riel, is that you be taken to the guard-room of the Mounted Police of Regina, whence you came, and kept there until September the eighteenth, and from thence to the place of execution, there to be hanged by the neck until dead, and may the Lord have mercy upon your soul!"

Riel never moved a muscle, but, bowing to the Court, said:—"Is that on Friday, your Honour?"

He was then taken from the Court-room, and a few minutes after was driven back, under strong escort, to the guard-room,

AN APPEAL.

After sentence had been passed upon Riel, Mr. Fitzgerald, one of prisoner's counsel, gave notice of appeal for a new trial to the Court of Queen's Bench, Manitoba. The appeal case was heard at Winnipeg on the 3rd and 4th days of September before Chief Justice Wallbridge and Mr. Justice T. W. Taylor.

M. LEMIEUX, chief counsel for Riel, raised the old issue as to informality of the trial before the Stipendiary Magistrate at Regina, and contended that the magistrate was incompetent to try the case.

Mr. FITZPATRICK followed. He held that the Treason-Felony Act was one of Imperial jurisdiction, and he questioned if it had delegated any power to the colonial authorities to legislate away any rights enjoyed by the subjects of the British Empire. He dwelt strongly upon the insanity question, and said the jury were convinced of the prisoner's lunacy, hence their recommendation to mercy.

Mr. EWART also strongly questioned the jurisdiction of the Court at Regina and cited several authorities in support of his argument.

Mr. ROBINSON, on behalf of the Crown, in an able address, strongly combated the idea that the Court at Regina was not legally constituted, and cited cases in support of his contention. He also dwelt at length on the insanity plea, showing the absurdity of the contention that Riel was insane.

Mr. Osler and Mr. Aikens followed on the same side, supplementing the arguments of the previous speaker as to the constitutionality of the Court, and cited a number of authorities adverse to the insanity plea.

NEW TRIAL REFUSED.

At Winnipeg, on the 9th September, at a sitting of the full Court of the Queen's Bench of the Province of Manitoba, judgment was delivered in the appeal for a new trial for the prisoner Riel.

His Lordship Chief Justice Wallbridge first delivered judgment. He referred briefly to the facts brought before the Court and the statutes by which the stipendiary magistrates are appointed in the North-West and to the powers given them for the trial of the cases before them alone, and to the cases, including treason, which have to be tried before a magistrate with a justice of the peace and a jury of six. His Lordship held that the constitutionality of the Court is established by the statutes passed, which he cited. If the Act passed by the Dominion Parliament was, as claimed by the defence, *ultra vires*, it was clearly confirmed by the Imperial Act subsequently passed, which made the Dominion Act equal to an Imperial Act. The objections were to his mind purely technical and therefore not valid. His opinion therefore was that a new trial should be refused, and the conviction of the Superior Court was therefore confirmed.

Mr. Justice Taylor followed, dealing fully with the arguments brought forward by the prisoner's counsel. On the question of the delegation of the power to legislate given to the Dominion Parliament, he held that the Dominion Parliament has plenary powers on all subjects committed to it. He reviewed fully all the facts relating to the admission of Rupert's Land to the Dominion, and to the statutes passed for the government of Rupert's Land and Manitoba when formed as a province. After a critical examination of the evidence in the case, he was unable to come to any other conclusion than that to which the jury had come. The evidence entirely fails to relieve the prisoner from responsibility for his acts. A new trial must be refused and the conviction must be confirmed.

Mr. Justice Killam next followed at some length, concurring in the views of his brother judges.

With these proceedings the trial of the rebel chief was concluded, though counsel for Riel has notified the Executive that they will appeal the case to the Privy Council in England. Riel will, meantime, be respited.

RIEL'S EXECUTION.

The execution of Louis David Riel took place at Regina, on the 16th November, 1885. He met his fate bravely, and displayed more fortitude than had been thought possible. He abstained from speech-making, and confined himself entirely, on the advice of Father Andre, who has been his constant companion throughout, to spiritual matters. Riel never slept after receiving intelligence that the execution would take place that morning, and throughout the night was constant in his devotions. At seven o'clock he had a light supper, and at five in the morning mass was celebrated, followed two hours later by the administration of the last sacrament. Riel, towards the last, almost entirely dropped his new religious idiosyncrasies and decided to die a devout catholic.

The hour fixed for the execution was eight o'clock, but it was fifteen minutes past that hour before those who had passes from the sheriff were admitted to the guard-room. Here was found the prisoner, kneeling on the floor of an upper room, from which he was to step to the gallows, It was a sad scene. Around him were gathered numbers of mounted police, Sheriff Chapleau, Deputy-Sheriff Gibson, and a few others. The room was illuminated by a small window, covered with a rime of frost through which the sun, now risen but a few hours, shot a few weak rays. Riel now knelt beside the open window, through which the gallows could be seen, and prayed incessantly for fully half an hour. Fathers McWilliams and Andre conducted the service for the doomed man in French, Riel repeating the responses in a clear voice, which could be heard distinctly above the murmurs of the priests' whispering tones. Riel wore a loose woollen surtout, grey trousers, and woollen shirt. On his feet were moccasins, the only feature of his dress that partook of the Indian that was in him. He received the notice to proceed to the scaffold in the same composed manner he had shown the preceding night on receiving warning of his fate. His face was full of colour, and he appeared to have complete self-possession, still responding to the service in a clear tone. The prisoner decided only a moment before starting for the scaffold not to make a speech. This was owing to the earnest solicitations of both the priests attending him. He displayed an inclination at the last moment to make an address, but Father Andre reminded him of his promise.

The hangman, who on a former occasion had been in the hands of Riel as a prisoner, commenced the work of pinioning the doomed man, and then the melancholy procession soon began to wend its way toward the scaffold, which had been erected for Khonnors, the Hebrew, and soon came in sight of the noose. Deputy-Sheriff Gibson went ahead, then came Father McWilliams, next Riel, then Father Andre, Dr. Jukes, and others. As he stood on the trap-door Riel continued invoking the aid of Jesus, Mary, and the saints, during his last agonies. "Courage, pere," he said, addressing Father Andre, and then he addressed Father McWilliams in the same words. The latter priest kissed Riel, who said, "I believe still in God."

"To the last," said Father Andre.

"Yes, the very last," answered Riel: "I believe and trust in Him. Sacred Heart of Jesus, have mercy on me."

Dr. Jukes shook hands with the prisoner, who said in
English: "Thank you, doctor." Then hle continued: "Jesus,
Marie, Joseph, assistez moi en ce dernier moment."

Deputy-Sheriff Gibson then said, "Louis Riel, have you anything to say before death?" Riel answered "No." He was given two minutes to pray, and he repeated the Lord's prayer, Father McWilliams leading, while the cap was being drawn over his face and the rope adjusted. At the words "Lead me not into temptation" the hangman sprang the bolt, at twenty-eight minutes past eight, and Riel shot downward with a terrible crash. For a second he did not move. A slight twitching of the limbs was noticed, but instantly all was still again. In two minutes after the fall, Louis Riel was no more. His conduct on the scaffold was very courageous. He was pale but firm, and kept up his courage by constant prayer, thus diverting his thoughts from the terrible death before him. His neck was broken by the fall; the doctors say he could have experienced no physical suffering. For a second or two his limbs twitched slightly, then a convulsive shudder ran through his frame, and all was over. In less than three minutes Dr. Dodds pronounced him dead.Few persons were present. The only people on the scaffold, besides the condemned man and the hangman, were Deputy-Sheriff Gibson, Dr. Jukes, of the Mounted Police, Father Andre, Father McWilliams, and the press representatives.After death the coroner's jury was empanelled by Dr Dodds, and a verdict of death by hanging rendered. The hair of the deceased was cut off one side of both head and face. All the buttons torn off the coat, the moccasins removed from the feet, and even the suspenders cut into pieces for persons to obtain mementos of the deceased. He was placed in a plain deal coffin to await the plans of the Government as to interment. His own wish was to be buried at St. Boniface, and his friends are particularly anxious that his wishes in this respect be complied with, as his father and other friends repose in that place, as all the bodies of the convicts here have been stolen from the burying ground in less than a week.

END

Milton Keynes UK
Ingram Content Group UK Ltd.
UKHW030908151124
451262UK00006B/916